SHOUT-OUTS FOR ISA CHANDRA MOSKOWITZ

ISA DOES IT

+ "This focused solo effort should enchant mainstreamers and the vegan-curious alike . . . For those who consider veganism a creed of abstinence and austerity, these joyous, vivid recipes are a persuasive argument to the contrary."
— *THE BOSTON GLOBE*

+ "Isa does it again! Delicious recipes that are explained in a way that a child could understand. Beautiful photos and mouthwatering, cruelty-free food! What more could you ask for?"
—EMILY DESCHANEL

+ "Isa Moskowitz has a peerless capacity to conjure comfort from the unique, transmute simple to divine, and, most importantly—she makes her vegan cooking prowess approachable. *Isa Does It*, like her other work, will be a dog-eared staple in my kitchen for years to come."
—BIZ STONE, FOUNDER OF TWITTER

+ "Moskowitz has singlehandedly revolutionized vegan cooking."
— *SAN FRANCISCO BOOK REVIEW*

+ "Isa Chandra Moskowitz comes to the rescue with her latest cookbook *Isa Does It*. The book is filled with pantry-friendly, satisfying recipes for every day of the week—and, yes, they're vegan, too!"
— *THE KITCHN*

+ "Warning: Food cravings are about to kick in."
— *WOMEN'S HEALTH*

+ "Veteran chefs, budding vegans, and bacon fanatics can all appreciate Moskowitz's hilarious prose, simple instructions, and culinary creativity."
— *PORTLAND MONTHLY*

+ "*Isa Does It* is full of her quips, making the book not only an unintimidating introduction to vegan cooking but also a darn fun read."
— *OMAHA MAGAZINE*

+ "Hands down, the best vegan cookbook of the year. Isa Chandra Moskowitz does it again with this collection of easy and delicious recipes designed for everyday cooking."
— *THE PORTLAND OREGONIAN*

VEGANOMICON (WITH TERRY HOPE ROMERO)

+ "[This] unassuming book is full of recipes for which even a carnivore would give up a night of meat."
— *SAN FRANCISCO CHRONICLE*

+ "Ever the clever wits, Moskowitz and Romero make gourmet vegan cooking accessible in *Veganomicon*. You'll love the menu suggestions at the back of the book and the massive index rivaling that of the *Joy of Cooking*."
— *CURVE*

+ "A must have."
  — *WASHINGTON TIMES*

+ "This cookbook takes the scariness out of vegan . . . The recipes are easy for new cooks to use and the book is user-friendly."
  —GWYNETH PALTROW ON GOOP.COM

+ "If you're considering transitioning to a vegan diet, or even just want to try it a day or two a week . . . [this is a] great introductory title."
  — *THE PORTLAND OREGONIAN*

+ "[The] magnum opus of vegan cookery."
  — *ATLANTA JOURNAL-CONSTITUTION*

APPETITE FOR REDUCTION

+ "From the grand dame of vegan cookbooks, *Appetite* doesn't leave you hungry . . . From salads that satisfy like meals to hearty pasta dishes to every vegetable imaginable, *Appetite* doesn't miss a beat."
  —*VEGNEWS*

+ "Moskowitz has singlehandedly revolutionized vegan cooking . . . *Appetite* is brimming not only with recipes, but also detailed nutritional information useful to everyone, but especially important to those who seek essential vitamins and nutrients from nontraditional (non-animal) sources. But if you're worried about typical bland diet food, have no fear: This is an Isa Chandra Moskowitz cookbook after all."
  —*SAN FRANCISCO BOOK REVIEW*

+ "[A] great read! . . . Moskowitz—a tireless crusader against the perception that meatless, dairy-free meals taste like cardboard—proves low-fat can be delicious. While offering plenty of tips for novice vegans, Moskowitz's recipes are interesting and flavorful enough to delight seasoned meatless mavens, too."
  —*NATURAL HEALTH*

+ "Bursting with inventive, flavorful techniques for lightening up comfort-food favorites and for making plants pop in new and exciting ways."
  —*BUST*

+ "This new book . . . is a winner for losers—weight losers, that is . . . Moskowitz offers delicious dishes that fill you up . . . There's no scrimping on nutrients or culinary creativity . . . Welcome to low-fat meals that are satisfying and mouthwatering, too."
  —*LIVING WITHOUT*

+ "[Moskowitz] begins with information on vegan nutrition and shares under-400-calorie recipes that are packed with flavor. Those new to a low-fat vegan diet may be surprised by satisfying meals such as OMG Oven-Baked Onion Rings, Chipotle Lentil Burgers with Sweet Potato Fries, Mac & Trees (macaroni, cheese, and broccoli), and Chili Verde con Papas."
  —*LIBRARY JOURNAL*

VEGAN *with a* VENGEANCE

**ALSO BY
ISA CHANDRA MOSKOWITZ**

ISA DOES IT

APPETITE FOR REDUCTION

VEGAN BRUNCH

**ALSO BY
ISA CHANDRA MOSKOWITZ
AND
TERRY HOPE ROMERO**

VEGANOMICON

VEGAN PIE IN THE SKY

VEGAN COOKIES INVADE YOUR COOKIE JAR

VEGAN CUPCAKES TAKE OVER THE WORLD

ISA CHANDRA MOSKOWITZ

PHOTOS BY KATE LEWIS

VEGAN *with a* VENGEANCE

OVER 150 DELICIOUS, CHEAP, ANIMAL-FREE RECIPES THAT ROCK

Celebrating **10 YEARS** OF VEGAN DOMINATION

Da Capo
LIFE
LONG

A Member of the Perseus Books Group

Photography © Kate Lewis
Food and prop styling by Kate Lewis
Studio assistants: Devin Echle & Melanie Buonavolonta

The following recipes were first published in *Vegan Cookies Invade Your Cookie Jar* by Isa Chandra Moskowitz
and Terry Hope Romero, Da Capo Press, 2009:

Peanut Butter Crisscrosses
Oatmeal Raisin Cookies
Kitchen Sink Chocolate Biscotti
Cranberry–White Chocolate Biscotti
Deluxe Cocoa Brownies
Call Me Blondies

The following recipes were first published in *Vegan Pie in the Sky* by Isa Chandra Moskowitz
and Terry Hope Romero, Da Capo Press, 2011:

Pumpkin Cheesecake with Praline Topping [originally published as Pumpkin Cheesecake]
Cosmos Apple Pie
Ginger Peach Pie

Editorial production by *Marra*thon Production Services. www.marrathon.net

Book Design by Megan Jones Design. www.meganjonesdesign.com
Set in 9 point Helvetica Neue LT Std

Cataloging-in-Publication data for this book is available from the Library of Congress.

Da Capo Press edition 2015

ISBN: 978-0-7382-1833-5 (paperback)

ISBN: 978-0-7382-1834-2 (e-book)

Published by Da Capo Press
A Member of the Perseus Books Group
www.dacapopress.com

Note: The information in this book is true and complete to the best of our knowledge. This book is intended only
as an informative guide for those wishing to know more about health issues. In no way is this book intended
to replace, countermand, or conflict with the advice given to you by your own physician. The ultimate decision
concerning care should be made between you and your doctor. We strongly recommend you follow his or her
advice. Information in this book is general and is offered with no guarantees on the part of the authors or Da Capo
Press. The authors and publisher disclaim all liability in connection with the use of this book.

Da Capo Press books are available at special discounts for bulk purchases in the U.S. by corporations, institutions,
and other organizations. For more information, please contact the Special Markets Department at the Perseus
Books Group, 2300 Chestnut Street, Suite 200, Philadelphia, PA, 19103, or call (800) 810-4145, ext. 5000, or
e-mail special.markets@perseusbooks.com.

10 9 8 7 6 5 4 3 2 1

DEDICATED TO THE MEMORY OF AMY SIMS.
SECOND BEST FRIEND. MATHLETE. RUNNING HEAVEN.

CONTENTS

<<< TEMPEH REUBEN, PAGE 105

COOKIES AND BARS

DESSERTS

INTRODUCTION

"I grew up cooking your recipes!" Standing before me at a book signing in an independent bookstore in Los Angeles is a fully grown adult woman with awesome bangs, a nose ring or two, and a huge smile, hugging a few of my cookbooks.

Well, how is that possible? She is a full-fledged taxpayer, obviously well into her twenties, and I'm . . . oh, god. I'm forty. Okay, fine, forty-something. I could probably be her mother or at least her very cool, favorite aunt.

But it makes sense. Maybe she means she was a toddler sitting on the kitchen counter while Mom and Dad (or Dad and Dad, or Mom and Mom or single Mom or single Dad, or other primary caregivers, whoever they may be) whipped up some *Vegan with a Vengeance* Scrambled Tofu.

Probably she means what I think of when I say "growing up." Those first adult moments went hand in hand with cooking. When I started sautéing onions and simmering chickpeas is also when I started becoming my own person, taking care of myself, and figuring out who I am; in the kitchen, and everywhere else, too. It's almost impossible for me to comprehend what this book meant to people. It's probably impossible for her—and you—to comprehend what these kinds of comments mean to me.

But let's start with easy, with the low-hanging fruit. Why a tenth-anniversary edition?

Well, ten is a nice round number. But also, so much has changed in the world, in my life, probably in *your* life, and in vegan cooking in general.

With ten years of cookbook authoring now under my pleather belt, I felt it was time to update some of these babies! Don't worry, I didn't mess with the super-beloved recipes; I just brought everything up to date and gave it all a little extra love. Here's a rundown:

EASIER DIRECTIONS

When I flip through *Vegan with a Vengeance*, I find revealing little glimpses into my former kitchen life. For instance, a lentil soup recipe that calls for the broth to be added in two stages. Why? Well, the truth is, I didn't have a pot big enough and had to wait for some of the water to evaporate before adding the rest. The quirks are cute, but not that practical. I've updated the directions in many recipes with the understanding that everyone has the right sized pot to make soup, and so forth.

STREAMLINED INGREDIENTS

Let me be honest: when I wrote *Vegan with A Vengeance*, I didn't want to use the same ingredients as everyone else; I also wanted to use *more* ingredients. This led to a few extra trips to the store for readers—and maybe reading glasses for the long lists. If a recipe had fewer than fifteen ingredients, I thought it must not be very good because anyone can make that! I didn't know that a great home cook can do a lot with very little. So now many ingredients lists are shorter but the results are just as delicious. I've also stopped using things like "vegan butter," so you'll find that, with a few exceptions, instead of nondairy substitutes as "nonhydrogenated vegan margarine," you'll find coconut oil or something equally yummy.

A FEW NEW RECIPES

I've also added a few new recipes that were favorites on my blog or that I thought would be perfect for people who are new to vegan cooking.

A FEW MAYBE NEW-TO-YOU RECIPES

Some of the added dessert recipes were pulled from the pages of the dessert trilogy I wrote with Terry Hope Romero (*Vegan Cupcakes Take Over the World, Vegan Cookies Invade Your Cookie Jar, and Vegan Pie in the Sky*). Why? Because they are basic things that everyone should be able to pull off, and there was no reason to reinvent the wheel for the perfect chocolate cupcake.

MORE FIZZLE

My cat, Fizzle, was about one year old when I started work on *Vegan with a Vengeance*. He is now twelve and still just a kitten to me! Oh, the things he has learned in the past decade. He is back (with a vengeance) with even more tips and knowledge than before. Look for "Fizzle says" throughout the book and become as much of a foodie as Fizzy is.

EXPERIMENT ALL YOU WANT

There is nothing mysterious going on—just follow the recipes and use my suggested substitutions if you need to. I remember once reading a Betty Crocker cookbook that asked readers not to deviate from a recipe—well, I say no such thing. Deviate all you want; recipes are mere guidelines. If the final dish tastes good to you, then it's a success.

NEW TO *VEGAN WITH A VENGEANCE?*

Of course, it's entirely possible that you have never seen a tattered copy of *Vegan with a Vengeance* in a college dorm kitchen, and you're, like, "Who in the world is this chick and what is she talking about?" Okay then! Here's the story.

Brooklyn 2001. I had just started a public access television show and website called *The Post Punk Kitchen*. The show was with my cohort and kitchen-sister, Terry. There wasn't much vegan cooking going on in the public sphere, and the show was needed but also a total blast. We threw together meals in my cramped (or cozy, depending on how you look at it) kitchen, while bands played and ate and had fun. It really was good clean punk rock fun, and we weren't expecting much beyond that.

But, ya know, you can't stop progress. A year or so into it, I got a call from a literary agent who had seen my interview in the (now defunct) zine *Punk Planet*. I had been working on a zine anyway and so a book deal sounded like not the worst idea.

Eight cookbooks later, here we are! I hope that if this cookbook is the start of your cooking journey, I'll see *you* in another ten years with *your* great bangs and tattered covers. Or your business casual attire. Or your walkers and bingo cards. Vegan cooking is for everyone!

It's been a privilege to be part of the vegan cookbook community for the past decade, and not a day goes by when I don't feel like the luckiest cool aunt in the world. Thank you for the opportunity.

Love always,
Isa

TOOLS AND KITCHEN STUFF

What a difference a decade makes! You'd think I'd have accumulated more and more stuff after all of these holidays and birthdays. But, no, I don't grab every single new gadget that comes on the market. I'll chop my avocado by hand, thank you very much, no avocado slicer needed. In fact, I've actually pared down my kitchen to the barest of necessities. Here are the tools I rely on.

CHEF'S KNIFE

I use my chef's knife for practically everything. If you are going to splurge on anything in the kitchen, I'd say forgo that fancy blender and just go straight for the chef's knife. One that you will have your entire life, which you can get professionally sharpened. And that feels comfortable in your hand. That being said, if you can't afford one of those at this point in your life, you can simply look on Amazon for the bestest, cheapo chef's knife, purchase that one, and put your dream knife on the wish list.

PARING KNIFE

I really could care less about the quality of my paring knife, but I definitely use it a lot, mostly for opening annoying plastic packaging or for slicing little things, like cherry tomatoes. There are really cute ones that come in leopard print or plaid, so I recommend style over function here because they are much more fun to Instagram.

SERRATED BREAD KNIFE

Sure, go ahead and get yourself one if you slice a lot of bread.

BIG, HEAVY WOOD CUTTING BOARD

Now that you can find a no-slip wooden cutting board with rubber grips on the bottom, there is no reason not to go wood or go home. Just remember to hand wash and dry it to keep it in top-notch condition. Oh, and wash immediately after slicing beets so you don't end up in the Pink Cutting Board Support Group.

MIXING BOWLS

You need three sizes: tiny, reasonable, and *OMG I will never need a mixing bowl this big*. Because, believe me, you will. Get a nice mix of vintage and stainless-steel ones and see which you use the most, just for fun.

CAST-IRON SKILLET

Stop being scared of cast iron! It will sear your veggies, brown your tofu, and caramelize your onions like nobody's business. Just make sure to hand wash with as little soap as possible and to dry immediately. Yes, I know, the Internet says not to wash with soap at all. But you know what? That's gross. And my cast-iron pans are still nonstick and awesome. So take that, Internet. Get a cast-iron grill pan as well, for those perfect grill marks.

SPATULAS AND SO FORTH

Forget those big plastic spatulas that look like a Doc Marten boot and will in no way, shape, or form be able to get underneath your seitan without the yummy browned parts sticking to the pan. Get thee a thin, flexible metal spatula. You'll also want a slanted wooden spatula for getting into the corners of your soup pot. And a rubber spatula for retrieving every last bit of brownie batter out of the mixing bowl.

LITTLE STAINLESS-STEEL SKILLET

For making frittatas and toasting small amounts of nuts or spices.

METAL TONGS

These are really an extension of your arm. Use them for tossing salads, flipping things, and grabbing things that are too high up on the shelves.

4-QUART STAINLESS-STEEL POT

Why is 4-quart the perfect size for almost everything? Think: pastas, soups, sauces. Heck, get two of these.

CERAMIC CASSEROLE DISH

For . . . casseroles!

RIMMED BAKING SHEETS

For roasting veggies and making sure that the juices don't overfloweth onto the bottom of the oven. I always line them with parchment so that I can keep them for a good long while. They are also great for baking cookies and scones!

PIZZA PAN

One with aeration holes, for perfect crisp crusts. And while you're at it, get a pizza stone, because why not?

MUFFIN TIN

Not only for muffins. For cupcakes, too.

MEASURING CUPS AND SPOONS

My prize possession is my 1¾-cup dry measuring cup. But you probably don't need that. You just need the basics: ¼, ⅓, ½, and 1 cup. And don't forget a 2-cup liquid measuring cup; if you have a lot of soup in your future, a 6-cup one is great to have, too. Metal measuring spoons that will fit inside your spice jars are priceless.

BLENDER

You don't *need* a high-speed super-power blender. But spend a few extra bucks to buy one whose motor won't burn out while you're making cashew cream.

FOOD PROCESSOR

Don't bother with a mini processor . . . if you're going to do it, do it right with a 12- or 14-cup model. You'll need it for pureeing with precision, and the grating attachment is perfect for when you don't want to give your arms a workout but you do need a lot of grated carrots.

IMMERSION BLENDER

For pureeing soups without having to transfer the whole shebang to a blender.

THE POST PUNK PANTRY

A well-stocked pantry is more of an ideal than a practical reality. I've compiled this list of what my mythical well-stocked pantry would contain, as a guide for you.

HERBS, SPICES, AND SEASONINGS

+ **PREGROUND SPICES:** allspice, anise, black pepper in a pepper mill, cardamom, cayenne, chile powder, Chinese five-spice, cinnamon, cloves, coriander, cumin, curry powder, ginger, nutmeg, paprika, turmeric

+ **WHOLE SPICES:** cardamom seeds, cinnamon sticks, cloves, coriander seeds, cumin seeds, fennel seeds, mustard seeds, nutmeg

+ **DRIED HERBS:** bay leaves, marjoram, oregano, rosemary, tarragon, thyme

GRAINS AND RICE

+ Arborio rice, basmati rice, vegan bread crumbs, brown rice, couscous (not technically a grain, but still), millet, vegan panko, quinoa

DRIED BEANS

+ Black-eyed peas, black beans, chickpeas (garbanzo beans), French lentils, navy beans, pinto beans, red lentils, split peas

NUTS (STORED IN THE FREEZER)

+ Almonds, untoasted cashews, hazelnuts, macadamia nuts, peanuts, pumpkin seeds, walnuts

CANNED GOODS

+ Black beans, chickpeas, canned coconut milk, pineapple juice, tomato paste, whole tomatoes in juice

NOODLES

+ Linguine, macaroni, rice noodles, soba noodles

BAKING STUFF

+ Almond extract, arrowroot, all-purpose flour, vegan baking chocolate (semisweet), baking powder, baking soda, vegan chocolate chips, unsweetened cocoa powder, shredded coconut, refined coconut oil, cornmeal, cornstarch, Dutch-processed cocoa powder, flaxseeds (whole or ground), lemon extract, maple extract, raisins, rolled oats, tapioca starch (also called tapioca flour), pure vanilla extract, whole wheat pastry flour

FROZEN FRUITS AND VEGGIES

+ Artichoke hearts, corn, edamame, peas, spinach, various berries and fruit

IN THE FRIDGE

+ Unsweetened almond milk (or your preferred nondairy milk), capers, Dijon mustard, tahini, tempeh, extra-firm tofu, Vegenaise (vegan mayonnaise), plain vegan yogurt

VINEGARS, OILS, AND LIQUID THINGS

+ Apple cider vinegar, balsamic vinegar, Bragg Liquid Aminos, brown rice syrup, canola oil, refined coconut oil, pure maple syrup, olive oil, peanut oil, rice wine vinegar, tamari or soy sauce, white cooking wine

OTHER VEGAN MUST-HAVES

+ Nutritional yeast, extra-firm silken tofu (vacuum-packed), vital wheat gluten

VEGANIZE IT!

Ten years ago, veganizing recipes was the biggest, most impossible challenge ever. I wrote this guide for my website when there was very little info out there. Nowadays, people throw around such words as *flax egg* without a care in the world, and many keep apple cider vinegar right on their baking shelf (if you don't know why, read on).

Still, this guide is a handy little thing if you want to make a family recipe vegan or if that cover cupcake on *Food Network Magazine* is calling your name but calls for four buckets of buttermilk and two farm-raised, biodynamic egg whites that have been kissed by Mother Teresa.

GET RID OF THE EGGS
EGGS

They bind. They leaven. They provide texture. They are arguably the most important ingredient in baking. But not all vegan versions are made equal. You can certainly play with these ingredients and find which is your spirit vegan egg, but these are my tried-and-true techniques. One caveat: if a recipe calls for more than two eggs (or three, tops), then I wouldn't recommend veganizing it. Just find a different recipe, because that recipe is probably too dependent on eggs, and I don't want you to risk wasting ingredients on something that won't come out well.

FLAXSEEDS

Golden flaxseeds are preferred because they blend right into light-colored batters, but any color flax will work the same. These days, it's easy to find ground flaxseed in the baking section or at least in the health food department of your local grocery store. Flaxseeds are a pretty wonderful ingredient, with magical binding properties when blended with liquid.

In the original version of this guide, I made distinctions between ground and whole flaxseeds, but I've grown a lot more relaxed these days. Because ground flaxseeds are so widely available, I just use ground.

HOW TO USE:

+ 1 tablespoon of ground flaxseeds plus 3 tablespoons of water or other liquid (such as vegan milk) replaces 1 egg. Either whiz in a small blender (such as a Magic Bullet) or beat together in a cup, using a fork. It will become very viscous, much like an egg white.

WHEN GROUND FLAXSEEDS WORK BEST:

Flax egg works very well in things like pancakes and such whole-grain items as bran or corn muffins. It's also my go-to for chewy cookies.

EXTRA-FIRM SILKEN TOFU

This is the vacuum-packed kind, found in shelf-stable packages, usually in the "ethnic" section of grocery stores. Mori-Nu is the most popular brand and works the best. I've changed my method for a tofu egg over the years and decided that if you're not replacing two eggs in a recipe, it's really not worth whipping up this concoction.

HOW TO USE:

+ ¼ cup of blended silken tofu plus ¼ cup of vegan milk = 1 egg. Whiz in a blender until completely smooth and creamy, leaving no graininess or chunks. You may need to add other wet ingredients to this mixture to get it to blend properly.

WHEN TOFU WORKS BEST:

Tofu egg works best in dense cakes and brownies and in smaller quantities for lighter cakes and fluffy things. Whizzed tofu leaves virtually no taste, so it is an excellent egg replacer in delicate cake recipes where flaxseeds would overpower the flavor. In cookie recipes, it may make the cookie more cake-like and fluffy than anticipated, so add 1 teaspoon of starch (such as arrowroot or cornstarch) right to the blender to combat that. Silken tofu may make pancakes a little heavy, so it is not recommended for those, although it could work well with a little experimentation.

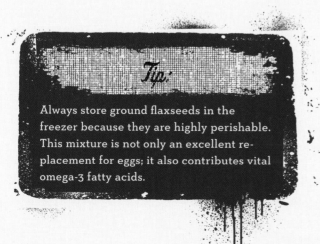

Tip:

Always store ground flaxseeds in the freezer because they are highly perishable. This mixture is not only an excellent replacement for eggs; it also contributes vital omega-3 fatty acids.

BANANA

Back in the '80s, when vegans would look at a banana tree, they probably thought that chickens were going to hatch from the fruit. This was, indeed, the only egg replacement I would ever use then. As you can imagine, all of my baked good tasted like banana. But I still love it! Bananas work wonders in baking, which is the reason many banana bread recipes don't require eggs. They hold the air bubbles well, make things nice and moist, and impart a nice flavor. If you don't go too overboard with it, the flavor isn't intrusive. Especially if it's in something chocolate.

HOW TO USE:

+ 1 ripe banana, mashed or processed into a puree = 2 eggs.

WHEN BANANA WORKS BEST:

Quick breads, muffins, cakes, and pancakes all taste perfect with a banana egg. I would recommend using this egg replacer in baked goods with assertive flavors, such as chocolate, gingerbread, orange, or carrot cakes, so that the banana flavor won't take over.

VEGAN YOGURT

How convenient! A container of vegan eggs, ready and waiting for you. There are so many different nondairy yogurts out there, but I haven't found a huge difference in how each works. I recommend coconut or soy yogurt, though, because those are also the funnest to eat. Yogurt works a lot like whizzed tofu as an egg replacer. It makes things moist and yummy.

HOW TO USE:

+ ¼ cup of plain, unsweetened vegan yogurt = 1 egg.

WHEN VEGAN YOGURT WORKS BEST:

Quick breads, muffins, cakes.

Tip

Make sure your bananas are nice and ripe and have started to brown.

APPLESAUCE

My baking shelf is stocked with those little lunch-box portion containers of applesauce. Is it the pectin that turns an apple into an egg? Jeez, I don't know. But who cares? It happens, and that's what matters. Use unsweetened for best results.

HOW TO USE:

+ ¼ cup of unsweetened applesauce = 1 egg.

WHEN APPLESAUCE WORKS BEST:

It's perfect in quick breads, Bundt cakes, scones, and muffins, but makes cookies a little too cakey.

Tip:

Those little containers I mentioned really are convenient. But they typically hold ⅓ cup of applesauce. Just look at it as a free bite of applesauce for the cook!

DO AWAY WITH DAIRY

MILK

This is a no-brainer, but there are soooo many vegan milks these days. My favorites? Unsweetened, unflavored almond or soy milk. I avoid such things as "coconut beverage" because it contains starches and thickeners that may make or break a recipe.

BUTTERMILK

HOW TO USE:

+ Add a teaspoon of apple cider vinegar to your vegan milk, and let it sit for a bit to curdle.

BUTTER

I've been moving further and further away from store-bought butter substitutes and closer and closer to one-ingredient oils. But not all oils are created the same!

Refined coconut oil is, by far, my favorite fat to use in baked goods. It's got a rich, almost buttery flavor. But I don't do a 1:1 replacement.

HOW TO USE:

+ Per ½ cup of butter called for in a recipe, substitute ⅓ cup of softened, room-temperature coconut oil plus 2 tablespoons of unsweetened applesauce. This will prevent greasiness and add a little lightness to all your baked goods.

BRUNCH

Brunch is probably my favorite meal in the world. I love waking up to the smell of onions and coffee and pancakes. In reality it's usually me doing the cooking and others waking up to it because I'm generous like that. But for whoever is doing the cooking, try to prep as much as you can the night before, so that you can roll out of bed and get things going.

⋘ "FRONCH" TOAST, PAGE 24

SCRAMBLED TOFU

1 tablespoon olive oil

1 medium-size yellow onion, chopped into ½-inch chunks

2 cups thinly sliced cremini mushrooms

2 to 3 cloves garlic, minced

1 pound extra-firm tofu, drained

¼ cup nutritional yeast

2 tablespoons freshly squeezed lemon juice

1 carrot, peeled (optional; I grate it in at the end, mostly for color)

FOR SPICE BLEND:

2 teaspoons ground cumin

1 teaspoon dried thyme, crushed with your fingers

1 teaspoon ground paprika

½ teaspoon ground turmeric

1 teaspoon salt

Fizzle says:

If you don't have nutritional yeast on hand, you can still make this recipe; just don't add any water when cooking.

Scrambled tofu was one of the first meals I tried to cook without a recipe, so you could say this is what started it all. To be honest, what I was trying to do was replicate the boxed mix you could buy at health food stores at the time!

This is a basic recipe but feel free to add a cup or so of any finely chopped vegetables that you want to use up. Broccoli, zucchini, and cauliflower are all great contenders; just add them when you add the mushrooms. Or you can fold in some spinach at the end along with the carrots. The most important thing is that you get the texture right; you want it to be chunky and not simply a mash. As you cook the tofu it will crumble more, so just break it into big chunks with your fingers right into the pan. This is a great-tasting way to introduce a tofuphobe to the heavenly bean curd we all know and love. Serve with Herb-Roasted Potatoes (page 21) or home fries, guacamole, and toast.

Heat a large, heavy-bottomed pan, preferably cast iron, over medium-high heat. Sauté the onion for 3 minutes in the tablespoon of olive oil, until softened. Add the mushrooms; sauté for 5 minutes, until soft and lightly browned. Add the garlic; sauté for 30 seconds or so, until fragrant. Mix in the spice blend. Add ¼ cup of water to deglaze the pan, scraping the bottom to get all the garlic and spices.

Crumble in the tofu and mix well, using a thin metal spatula. Don't crush the tofu; just kind of lift it and mix it around. You want it to remain chunky.

Let cook for about 15 minutes, stirring occasionally and adding splashes of water, if necessary, to keep it from sticking too much. Lower the heat a bit if you find that the tofu is sticking. Add the nutritional yeast and lemon juice and toss to combine.

Grate the carrot, if using, into the tofu mixture and fold in. Taste for salt and seasonings, and serve!

VARIATIONS:

TOFU RANCHEROS: Add 1 cup of salsa at the end; cook for 1 minute extra.

ASIAN-STYLE SCRAMBLED TOFU: Add 2 tablespoons of minced fresh ginger with the garlic, use peanut oil instead of olive oil, substitute shiitake mushrooms, and omit the thyme and nutritional yeast. Mix in 1 cup of thinly sliced scallions at the very end, along with carrot.

 *Fizzle says:*

Using a cast-iron pan and a very thin, metal spatula is the best way to make sure your tofu gets nice and brown and that you get all the delicious bits of flavor that might stick to the bottom of the pan.

ASPARAGUS AND SUN-DRIED TOMATO FRITTATA

1 pound extra-firm tofu

1 tablespoon soy sauce

1 teaspoon Dijon mustard (yellow will work fine if you like that better)

¼ cup nutritional yeast

2 teaspoons olive oil

½ cup onion (1 small), cut into ¼-inch dice

3 stalks asparagus, rough ends discarded, cut into bite-size pieces

¼ cup sun-dried tomatoes packed in oil, finely chopped

2 cloves garlic, minced

1 teaspoon dried thyme

¼ teaspoon ground turmeric

2 tablespoons freshly squeezed lemon juice

¼ cup fresh basil leaves, torn into pieces

A frittata is an open-faced, baked omelet. I love the combo of asparagus and sun-dried tomatoes for its colors as well as taste and texture, but you can get creative with your vegetable choices or use some of my variations below. No need to press the tofu; just drain it and give it a squeeze over the sink—that oughta do it.

Preheat the oven to 400°F.

In a mixing bowl, mash the tofu until it resembles ricotta cheese. This should take about a minute. Mix in the soy sauce and mustard. Add the nutritional yeast and combine well. Set aside.

Heat an oven-safe 8-inch skillet over medium heat. Sauté the onion in the olive oil for 2 minutes. Add the asparagus and sun-dried tomatoes; sauté for about 3 more minutes. Add the garlic, thyme, and turmeric; sauté for 1 more minute. Add the lemon juice to deglaze the pan; turn off the heat. Transfer the onion mixture to the tofu mixture and combine well. Fold in the basil leaves. Transfer back to the skillet and press the mixture firmly in place. Cook in the oven at 400°F for 20 minutes. If you like, transfer to the broiler to brown the top, about 2 minutes (keep a close eye on it so as not to burn it). Let the frittata sit for 10 minutes before serving. Cut into four slices and lift each piece out with a pie server to prevent the frittata from falling apart. If it does crumble a bit, don't fret; just put it back into shape.

Fizzle says:

If you don't have an 8-inch skillet, then employ an 8-inch pie plate when baking the frittata.

VARIATIONS:

BROCCOLI AND OLIVE FRITTATA: Replace the asparagus with ½ cup of chopped broccoli florets. Replace the sun-dried tomatoes with sliced black olives.

INDIAN FRITTATA: Replace the asparagus with ½ cup of chopped cauliflower florets. Replace the sun-dried tomatoes with ¼ cup of cooked chickpeas. Omit the thyme and basil; add 1 teaspoon of curry powder and 1 teaspoon of ground cumin.

MUSHROOM FRITTATA: Sauté 1 cup of sliced cremini mushrooms along with the onion. Omit the asparagus; use ¼ cup of sliced black olives or sun-dried tomatoes. Serve with Mushroom Sauce (page 93).

TEMPEH AND WHITE BEAN SAUSAGE PATTIES

MAKES 10 PATTIES

1 pound tempeh, crumbled into bite-size pieces

4 teaspoons Braggs Liquid Aminos or soy sauce

1 cup cooked white beans

3 tablespoons olive oil

2 cloves garlic, minced

1 teaspoon whole fennel seeds, crushed (see Fizzle says, page 17)

1 heaping tablespoon chopped fresh thyme

1 heaping teaspoon chopped fresh sage (about 5 leaves)

Pinch of ground cayenne pepper

Pinch of ground nutmeg

1 tablespoon tomato paste

1/4 cup plain vegan bread crumbs

Dash of salt

A few dashes of freshly ground black pepper

White beans and tempeh go together naturally. The beans have a naturally smoky flavor, and the tempeh and herbs give these patties the savory taste I crave upon rolling out of bed on a Sunday morning or (let's be honest) afternoon. They have a softer texture than store-bought vegetarian sausage patties but a much better flavor. You can prepare the mix up to two days in advance so that all you have to do the day of serving is form the patties and cook.

Place the tempeh into a saucepan and just barely cover with water (it's okay, even preferable, if some of the tempeh is peeking out of the water). Add 1 teaspoon of the Bragg's, cover, and bring to a boil. Simmer for about 15 minutes, or until most of the water is absorbed. Drain any remaining water and transfer the tempeh to a large bowl. Add the white beans, give a quick stir, and set aside. This will heat the beans just a bit for easier mashing and cool the tempeh down just a bit for easier handling.

Give the saucepan a quick rinse and dry. Sauté the garlic and fennel seeds in 1 tablespoon of the olive oil over low heat, just until fragrant, about 1 minute. Add the remainder of the spices and stir constantly for 30 seconds. Add to the tempeh mixture along with the tomato paste and remaining tablespoon of Bragg's.

Mash everything together with a potato masher or strong fork until it's just a bit chunky and there are no whole beans left (you don't want it pureed; you should still be able to see the beans). Add the bread crumbs and combine well. Taste for salt and spices and adjust to your liking. Refrigerate for about 15 minutes to allow the flavors to meld and to help the sausages to bind.

Form into patties, using about 3 tablespoons' worth of the mix (you can use a quarter-cup measuring cup filled three-quarters full to make the patties consistent in size). Heat the remaining 2 tablespoons of olive oil in a pan over medium heat. Cook the patties until browned, about 3 minutes each side. You may need to add a little more oil when you flip them over.

BREAKFAST LENTIL CHORIZO

SPICE MIX:

2 teaspoons mild chili powder

1 teaspoon chipotle powder

1 teaspoon ground cumin

1 teaspoon fennel seed, crushed

½ teaspoon dried oregano

½ teaspoon salt

CHORIZO:

2 teaspoons olive oil

1 small onion, minced

2 cloves garlic, minced

2½ cups cooked lentils
(from about 1 cup dried)

3 tablespoons tomato paste

2 tablespoons fresh squeezed
lemon juice

This is what you want to serve alongside your scrambled tofu when you're looking for a smoky, Mexican-inspired twist. A little guacamole and salsa and you're good to go. But don't stop there! It also makes a great sandwich, or a burger topping, or a taco filling.

First combine all of the ingredients for the spice mix and set aside. Also, keep a cup of water within reach, you'll need to add splashes as you cook.

Preheat a large skillet over medium-high heat. Sautee the onion and garlic in the oil with a pinch of salt for about 3 minutes, until lightly browned. Add spices and toss them for 30 seconds or so to toast.

Lower heat to medium, add lentils, a few splashes of water, tomato paste, and lemon juice. Use a spatula to mash them a bit as they cook, until they hold together. If your spatula isn't strong enough to accomplish this, just use a fork. Do this for about 5 minutes, adding splashes of water as necessary if it appears dry. Taste for salt and seasoning and serve.

 *Fizzle says:*

To quickly crush the seeds, place them in a coffee grinder and pulse three or four times. If you are too punk for a coffee grinder, place the seeds in a plastic bag and cover with a thin towel or even a few pieces of newspaper, and proceed to hammer with a mallet or a regular hammer until the neighbors complain. You can also use a rolling pin to roll over the plastic bag until the seeds are good and crushed.

TEMPEH SAUSAGE CRUMBLES

1 (8-ounce) package tempeh

2 tablespoons whole fennel seeds, crushed (see Fizzle says, page 17)

1 teaspoon dried basil

1 teaspoon dried marjoram or oregano

½ teaspoon red pepper flakes

½ teaspoon dried sage

2 cloves garlic, minced

2 tablespoons tamari or soy sauce

1 tablespoon olive oil

Juice of ½ lemon

This is still a favorite of mine! When I first began writing this book, I wasn't sure what section to put this recipe into because I use it in so many different kinds of meals—in pasta sauce, in gravy, as a side dish for brunch, or as a pizza topping. I decided to put it here, but don't be afraid to experiment with it. I did make a few adjustments over the years, mostly using a little fewer fennel seeds and crushing it to bring out the flavor.

In a small pan, crumble the tempeh and add enough water to almost cover it. Over medium-high heat, simmer the tempeh until most of the water is absorbed, 12 to 15 minutes. Drain the remaining water, add the rest of the ingredients, and cook over medium heat, stirring occasionally, until lightly browned, about 10 minutes.

TEMPEH BACON

3 tablespoons Bragg Liquid Aminos or tamari or soy sauce

⅓ cup apple juice or cider

1 teaspoon tomato paste

1 teaspoon liquid smoke

1 (8-ounce) package tempeh

2 cloves garlic, crushed

2 tablespoons peanut or vegetable oil

I love these smoky strips alongside pancakes, or in a TLT or in a salad or in a house or with a mouse. They aren't going to fool any meat eaters, but they'll fully satisfy us herbivores. You need to marinate the tempeh for a good hour, so plan ahead or marinate it overnight. Peanut oil adds a richer flavor, so I recommend using it, but canola or vegetable oil will do nicely. You can use thinly sliced, pressed tofu if you haven't got any tempeh. One difference in this recipe from the original is that I slice the tempeh widthwise instead of lengthwise, because it takes a lot less skill and there is no risk of the strips' breaking in half. Another is that I upped the liquid smoke from ¼ teaspoon to 1 whole teaspoon because SMOKINESS!

Fizzle says:

These tempeh strips are perfect for TLTs! Get some white bread, crunchy romaine, and gorgeous heirloom tomatoes. Slather on some mayo and you are golden.

To make the marinade, combine the Bragg's, cider, tomato paste, and liquid smoke in a wide, shallow bowl and mix with a fork until the tomato paste is fully dissolved. Set aside.

Cut the tempeh into ¼-inch-thick strips widthwise. Rub the strips with the crushed garlic, then toss the garlic cloves into the marinade. Submerge the tempeh strips in the marinade and let sit, turning occasionally, for at least an hour and up to overnight. After marinating, discard the garlic.

Heat the peanut oil in a large skillet over medium heat. Add the tempeh strips and cook for 4 minutes on one side; the bottom should be nicely browned. Flip the strips over and pour the remainder of the marinade over them; if there isn't much marinade left, add a splash of water. Cover and let cook for 3 more minutes, until the liquid is absorbed. Uncover and keep cooking until all sides are nicely browned, 5 minutes or so. Remove from the heat and serve.

3 tablespoons olive oil

1 medium-size onion, cut into ¼-inch dice

2 cloves garlic, minced

¼ teaspoon salt

1½ teaspoons Chinese five-spice powder

3 medium-size sweet potatoes, cut into ½-inch dice

1 bunch watercress, stems discarded, torn into big pieces

I whipped this up one morning to go with my scrambled tofu when the only vegetables I had around were sweet potatoes and peppery watercress. The watercress made me think Chinese, and the Chinese made me think five-spice powder and thus this simple but delicious creation was born. The watercress does a great job of picking up the spices and the garlic.

In a large skillet over medium-high heat, cook the onion in 1 tablespoon of the olive oil for 2 minutes, stirring occasionally. Add the garlic, salt, and five-spice and cook for about 1 minute. Add the sweet potatoes and the rest of the oil. Cook for 12 to 15 minutes, until the potatoes are cooked and caramelized a bit. Add the watercress and cook, stirring constantly, for 2 more minutes.

Fizzle says:

Chinese five-spice powder incorporates the five basic tastes of Chinese cooking—sweet, sour, bitter, umami (pungent), and salty. The blend commonly sold in America consists of cinnamon, black pepper, cloves, fennel seeds, and star anise.

HERB-ROASTED POTATOES

3 pounds small red potatoes, halved widthwise

1 medium-size onion, quartered and sliced ½ inch thick

¼ cup olive oil

2 teaspoons coarse sea salt

Several dashes of freshly ground black pepper

4 teaspoons fresh rosemary, chopped

4 teaspoons chopped fresh thyme

You can't have brunch without potatoes—I'd like to see you try. I love these crispy, salty spuds and they are all kinds of easy to prepare. I like to make them with baby potatoes because there is much less prep work and I just find the shape pleasing. But you can also cut the potato into 1¼-inch chunks. I adjusted the time a little bit from the original recipe because my oven must have been way off in that tiny Brooklyn apartment. It doesn't take an hour to roast potatoes at high heat. Silly me.

Preheat the oven to 450°F. Divide the potatoes and onion between two rimmed baking pans or a large rimmed baking sheet, sprinkle with oil and then salt and pepper, and toss to coat (I find it's easiest to use your hands for this). Roast for 20 minutes.

Remove from the oven, sprinkle with the herbs, toss to coat (use a spatula now, they're hot! I'm sure you realize this but just in case . . .). Return to the oven and roast until browned and tender, about 20 minutes longer.

BAKING POWDER BISCUITS AND WHITE BEAN TEMPEH SAUSAGE GRAVY

2 cups all-purpose flour

5 teaspoons baking powder

1 teaspoons salt

3 tablespoons nonhydrogenated shortening

2 tablespoons nonhydrogenated vegan margarine

⅔ cup unsweetened almond milk (or preferred nondairy milk)

This biscuit recipe is adapted from a 1944 cookbook entitled *Ruth Wakefield's Toll House Tried and True Recipes*. In her introduction she states, "I know there are no substitutions for butter, cream, eggs, fresh fruits and vegetables for preparing a fine meal." I agree with the fruit and veggies part but aside, from that I have thoroughly ignored Ruth's advice and her modified biscuit recipe has served me well for years. If you'd like, you can serve these with the White Bean and Tempeh Sausage Gravy (recipe follows) or the Mushroom Sauce on page 93, or ignore my suggestions as I did Ruth's and serve them with margarine or whatever else you want. The gravy is a modified version of a recipe submitted to my website by someone named Lisa over ten years ago. Thanks, Lisa.

Preheat the oven to 450°F. Lightly grease a cookie sheet.

Sift together the flour, baking powder, and salt. Cut the shortening and margarine into the flour with a pastry knife or your fingers. Add the milk to form a soft dough. Mix well and pat out on a floured countertop until about ½ inch thick; cut out 2-inch rounds with the rim of a glass or cookie cutter. Place on the prepared cookie sheet and bake for 12 to 15 minutes, until risen and lightly browned.

WHITE BEAN AND TEMPEH SAUSAGE GRAVY

Tempeh Sausage Crumbles
(page 18)

2 cups cooked white beans
(or 1 [15-ounce] can, drained
and rinsed)

2 tablespoons olive oil

¼ cup vegan vegetable broth
or water

½ teaspoon salt

A few dashes of freshly ground
black pepper

10 to 12 leaves fresh sage, chopped

Here's that white bean and tempeh combo again. It really does scream "gravy!" This recipe was the first gravy I ever made. It's got succulent bits of tempeh that mimic sausage, and the pureed white beans provide a nice, hearty, but creamy base.

Prepare the Tempeh Sausage Crumbles and keep them warm in the pan.

Puree the white beans with the olive oil and broth in a blender or food processor until relatively smooth. Add to the tempeh crumbles along with the salt and pepper. Heat through for a few minutes. If you want to make the gravy thinner, add a little more broth. Mix in the sage and cook for another 2 minutes.

"FRONCH" TOAST

Loaf of day-old Italian bread (enough for 12 [1-inch] slices)

1 cup unsweetened almond milk (or preferred nondairy milk)

2 tablespoons organic cornstarch

¼ cup chickpea flour

Several tablespoons of refined coconut oil

This recipe is still the Fronchiest and toastiest, even though I made a few adjustments. I couldn't tell you what it is about chickpea flour but this French toast looks and tastes just like the "real" thing. These days, I prefer to use a soft Italian bread as my toast. In the original recipe I used vegetable oil for cooking, but now I always use refined coconut oil. It has such a buttery and rich taste, it takes this already favorite recipe to even new heights. I also ditched the soy creamer in the recipe, opting for more streamlined almond milk. Serve with fresh berries, sliced bananas, and pure maple syrup.

Slice the bread into 1-inch rounds.

Pour the milk into a wide, shallow bowl. Mix in the cornstarch and stir until dissolved. Add the chickpea flour and mix until it is mostly absorbed; some lumps are okay.

Heat a large, heavy-bottomed pan, preferably cast iron, over medium-high heat. Add enough oil to create a thin layer on the bottom (a tablespoon or two).

Soak the bread slices (as many as will fit into your pan) in the mixture and transfer to the skillet. Cook each side for about 2 minutes; if they are not browned enough when you flip them, heat for 1 or 2 more minutes on each side. They should be golden brown with flecks of dark brown. Serve immediately.

Fizzle says:

Really, this works with any bread. It works best if it's day old, but if you're using sliced bread from a package, lightly toast it first to prevent sogginess, and you're all set!

PERFECT PANCAKES

There is nothing like a stack of pancakes dripping with maple syrup, served with some smoky tempeh bacon on the side. Although pancake ingredients are fairly simple, the combination of flour and water seems to have an uncanny ability to stress a person out. I'm no motivational speaker, but trust me—it may take a couple of tries to get perfect pancakes, but you can do it. Here are some tips to guide you along the way. (If it helps, picture my head in a dream cloud floating above your left shoulder, guiding you on. If that doesn't help and only serves to freak you out, then just follow these guidelines.)

+ The amount of water you need depends on several factors, including altitude and the humidity in the air on any given day. I suggest using the liquid quantities I give as a guideline. First, add 1 cup of milk. If the batter looks too thick, or if your first pancake doesn't bubble up, add the remaining liquid.

+ Don't overmix the batter. You want a couple of lumps in the flour; overmixed batter results in rubbery pancakes.

+ You may notice that pancakes get lighter and fluffier as you get to the end of the batter. That's because the gluten in the flour has had some time to relax. Let your pancake batter sit for 10 minutes or so before proceeding.

+ Make sure your pan is nonstick. If it's cast iron, which I think is the best for pancakes, make sure it's well seasoned.

+ The pan should be hot enough, but not smoking. After preheating the pan, flick a couple of drops of water in. The drops should bounce but not sizzle up and evaporate immediately. You can also do a test with a tablespoon of batter.

+ Don't go crazy with the grease. A very thin coating of oil will do it. Use a spray bottle of canola oil for an even coating. Apply a fresh coat every time you start a new batch.

+ To form your pancakes into perfect circles, use the same amount of batter in a ladle every time. Pour the batter out with a slightly circular motion, so that it spreads evenly. Don't just plop it down or the middle will be thicker than the edges. You can also try using a meat baster; just fill it up and squeeze the pancake batter out. You'll be amazed at the perfect circles this creates. And you aren't using that meat baster for anything gross like meat, anyway.

+ The most important thing is that you don't give up. Some say the first pancake is always a flop, so just keep trying. You will get the hang of it!

PANCAKES

1¼ cups all-purpose flour

2 teaspoon baking powder

½ teaspoon salt

1 to 1¼ cups unsweetened almond milk (or preferred nondairy milk)

2 tablespoons pure maple syrup

2 tablespoons canola oil, plus oil for the pan

1 teaspoon pure vanilla extract

VARIATIONS:

Add these after the basic batter's been mixed:

RASPBERRY LIME: Fold in 1 cup of fresh raspberries and 1 tablespoon of finely grated lime zest.

BLUEBERRY: Fold in 1 cup of fresh blueberries.

MISH'S FAVORITE: Fold in ½ cup of vegan semisweet chocolate chips.

S traight up pancakes, just like at the diner at two a.m. If you have extreme pancake fear and intimidation (burned tops and bottoms and runny insides), follow the tips for Perfect Pancakes and you can't go wrong!

In a large mixing bowl, sift together the flour, baking powder, and salt. Make a well in the center and add ⅓ cup of water, 1 cup of the milk, and the maple syrup, oil, and vanilla. Mix until just combined, adding up to ¼ cup more milk, if necessary. Do not overmix or the pancakes will be tough; a couple of lumps are okay.

Heat a large, heavy-bottomed non-stick pan, preferably cast iron, over medium heat. Let the pan heat while the batter rests.

Add a thin layer of oil to the pan, and cook the pancakes until browned on the bottom and bubbles form on top, about 4 minutes. Turn the pancakes over and cook until the bottoms are browned and the pancakes are barely firm to touch. Repeat with the remaining batter, adding more oil to the pan as needed.

COCONUT PANCAKES
WITH PINEAPPLE SAUCE

1¼ cups all-purpose flour

2 teaspoons baking powder

½ teaspoon salt

1 teaspoon ground or freshly grated nutmeg (if using fresh, it's ⅓ of a whole nutmeg)

1 to 1¼ cups unsweetened almond milk (or preferred nondairy milk)

2 tablespoons pure maple syrup

1 teaspoon pure vanilla extract, or use coconut extract if you have it on hand

2 tablespoons coconut or canola oil, plus oil for the pan

1 cup unsweetened shredded coconut

To transform your kitchen into a tropical paradise, serve these pancakes with Pineapple Sauce (recipe follows) which is ridiculously easy to make. I love scraping fresh nutmeg into the batter; it makes me feel like a real homemaker. And it goes so perfectly with coconut.

Sift together the flour, baking powder, salt, and nutmeg. Create a well in the center of the dry ingredients; add ⅓ cup of water, 1 cup of the milk, and the maple syrup, vanilla, and oil. Mix until just combined, adding up to ¼ cup more milk, if necessary; fold in the coconut.

Heat a large, heavy-bottomed nonstick pan, preferably cast iron, over medium heat, while the batter rests.

Add a thin layer of oil to the pan. If making large pancakes, use a ladle to pour the batter into the pan; most standard ladles will yield a 6-inch pancake. For smaller pancakes, drop the batter by ¼ cupfuls into the pan. Cook until bubbles form on top, about 3 minutes. Turn the pancakes over and cook until the bottoms are browned and the pancakes are cooked through, about 2 more minutes. Serve immediately or keep warm on a plate covered with foil while you cook the others. Serve with pineapple sauce.

PINEAPPLE SAUCE

MAKES 2 CUPS

1 (20-ounce) can pineapple chunks in juice

2 tablespoons arrowroot powder

3 tablespoons sugar

1 teaspoon pure vanilla extract

In a saucepan, off the heat, stir the pineapple and juice with the arrowroot until it is mostly dissolved; stir in the sugar. Over medium heat, heat the pan until the sauce thickens, stirring often, about 7 minutes. Stir in the vanilla.

BANANA-PECAN PANCAKES

MAKES 9 SMALL PANCAKES

1½ cups all-purpose flour

1½ teaspoons baking powder

½ teaspoon baking soda

¼ teaspoon salt

⅛ teaspoon ground cinnamon

1¼ cups very well-mashed banana

1½ cups unsweetened almond milk
(or preferred nondairy milk)
plus 1 teaspoon vinegar
(let sit for 5 minutes)

1 tablespoon canola oil

1 teaspoon pure vanilla extract

½ cup pecans, chopped

Canola oil or cooking spray
for the pan

I called these Banana-Pecan Pancakes just to get your attention; the truth is you can use any nut you like, or even vegan chocolate chips instead. Banana provides great flavor, and of course also makes for a wonderful, fluffy pancake. I made a vow not to use the word *crowd-pleaser* in this cookbook but I am going to sell out and tell you—these are a great crowd-pleaser! Everyone loves them. These cook up thicker than the other pancake recipes, so I recommend making smaller pancakes and cooking them three to a pan. Serve with additional bananas and strawberries, too!

Sift together the flour, baking powder, baking soda, salt, and cinnamon.

In a separate bowl, mix the mashed banana with the milk, oil, and vanilla until pretty smooth. Pour the wet ingredients into the dry and mix, but do not overmix. Fold in the pecans.

Heat a large, heavy-bottomed nonstick pan, preferably cast iron, over medium heat. Let the pan heat while the batter rests.

Add a thin layer of oil to the pan. Working in batches of three, pour ⅓ cup of batter per pancake into the pan and cook until bubbles appear on the surface and the undersides are golden brown, about 3 minutes. Flip the pancakes with a spatula and cook until golden brown and cooked through, about 2 minutes more. Serve immediately or keep warm on a plate covered with foil while you cook the others.

CHOCOLATE–CHOCOLATE CHIP PANCAKES

1 cup plus 2 tablespoons all-purpose flour

3 tablespoons unsweetened cocoa powder

2 teaspoons baking powder

½ teaspoon salt

1 to 1¼ cups unsweetened almond milk (or preferred nondairy milk)

2 tablespoons canola oil

3 tablespoons pure maple syrup

1 teaspoon pure vanilla extract

⅓ cup vegan semisweet chocolate chips

Canola oil or cooking spray for the pan

I know. Chocolate for breakfast. Reserve this one for special occasions like Valentine's Day, or don't, just go ahead and be decadent. Serve with Strawberry Sauce (page 255) or fresh raspberries and maple syrup.

In a large mixing bowl, sift together the flour, cocoa powder, baking powder, and salt. Create a well in the center of the flour mixture and add ⅓ cup of water, 1 cup of the milk, and the oil, maple syrup, and vanilla. Mix until just combined, adding up to ¼ cup more milk, if necessary; fold in the chocolate chips.

Heat a large, heavy-bottomed, non-stick pan, preferably cast iron, over medium-high heat.

If making large pancakes, use a ladle to pour the batter into the pan; most standard ladles will yield a 6-inch pancake. For smaller pancakes, drop the batter by ⅓ cupfuls into the pan. Cook until bubbles form on top, about 3 minutes. Turn the pancakes over and cook until the bottoms are browned and the pancakes are cooked through, about 2 more minutes. Serve immediately or keep warm on a plate covered with foil while you cook the others. Repeat with the remaining batter.

GINGER-PEAR WAFFLES

MAKES EIGHT 6-INCH ROUND WAFFLES

2 cups all-purpose flour

2 teaspoons baking powder

1 teaspoon baking soda

½ teaspoon salt

2 teaspoons ground ginger

½ teaspoon ground cinnamon

¼ teaspoon ground allspice

¼ teaspoon ground or freshly grated nutmeg

1 cup pear or apple juice

¾ cup unsweetened almond milk (or preferred nondairy milk)

⅓ cup unsweetened applesauce

2 tablespoons canola oil

3 tablespoons sugar

2 teaspoons pure vanilla extract

1 pear, grated

These are the best autumn waffles. You can use whatever pears look best at the farmers' market; just make sure they're little underripe, for easy grating. And don't worry about peeling the pear; the skin adds a nice texture and interesting flecks of color. Serve with additional slices of pear fanned on top, and if you'd like a little extra gingeriness, chop up some crystallized ginger for garnish. Fancy!

Preheat a waffle iron according to the manufacturer's directions.

In a large mixing bowl, sift together the flour, baking powder, baking soda, salt, and spices in a large mixing bowl. In a medium-size bowl, mix together the juice, milk, applesauce, oil, sugar, and vanilla until well combined. Create a well in the center of the flour mixture and slowly blend the wet ingredients into the dry until combined. Fold in the grated pear.

Make your waffles according to the manufacturer's directions, spraying or brushing the iron with oil between each waffle. Keep warm on a plate covered with foil until ready to serve.

LEMON-CORN WAFFLES WITH BLUEBERRY-MAPLE SAUCE

MAKES EIGHT 6-INCH ROUND WAFFLES

1½ cups all-purpose flour

2 teaspoons baking powder

1 teaspoon baking soda

½ teaspoon salt

¾ cup cornmeal

2 cups unsweetened almond milk (or preferred nondairy milk)

¼ cup canola oil

¼ cup plain vegan yogurt

¼ cup freshly squeezed lemon juice

2 teaspoons lemon zest

¼ cup sugar

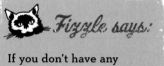

Fizzle says:

If you don't have any yogurt, unsweetened applesauce is a fine substitution!

Lemon + corn = heaven. Lemon + corn + blueberries = the VIP section of heaven. You can even up the ante by drizzling a little Macadamia Crème (page 255) over the Blueberry-Maple Sauce (recipe follows). These were the biggest waffle hit from the original edition! I made a few little tweaks just to ensure consistent results.

Preheat a waffle iron according to the manufacturer's directions.

Sift together the flour, baking powder, baking soda, salt, and cornmeal in a large mixing bowl. Create a well in the center and add the milk, oil, yogurt, lemon juice, zest, and sugar. Mix together to combine, being careful not to overmix.

Make your waffles according to the manufacturer's directions, spraying or brushing the iron with oil between each waffle. Keep warm on a plate covered with foil until ready to serve.

BLUEBERRY-MAPLE SAUCE

MAKES 3 CUPS SAUCE

1½ tablespoons organic cornstarch

1 pound frozen blueberries, partially thawed

½ cup pure maple syrup

1 teaspoon pure vanilla extract

In a small saucepan off the heat, toss the cornstarch with the blueberries until it is mostly dissolved. This takes about 5 minutes; mix occasionally.

Over medium heat, cook until moisture is released and the blueberries are warm. Add the maple syrup and vanilla; heat for 5 more minutes, until the sauce thickens a bit.

OATMEAL-BANANA-RAISIN WAFFLES

1 cup plus 2 tablespoons
all-purpose flour

2 teaspoons baking powder

1 teaspoon baking soda

1¼ teaspoons ground cinnamon

¼ teaspoon ground nutmeg

½ teaspoon salt

1 cup rolled oats

1 very ripe medium-size banana

1½ cups unsweetened almond milk
(or preferred nondairy milk)

3 tablespoons pure maple syrup

3 tablespoons canola oil

¾ cup raisins

Extra sliced bananas for the top

I love the texture the oatmeal gives these waffles. They are chewy and have a hint of banana and cinnamon, with sweet bursts of raisins. Good, wholesome, delicious fun! Serve with extra sliced banana and raisins, and if you're feeling extra fancy, throw on a raspberry or two for color.

Preheat a waffle iron according to the manufacturer's directions.

In a mixing bowl, sift together the flour, baking powder, baking soda, cinnamon, nutmeg, and salt. Add the oatmeal and toss together.

In a separate bowl, mash the banana very well. Add the milk, maple syrup, and oil. Mix vigorously with a strong fork until very few clumps of banana are left. Add the wet ingredients to the dry and mix just until combined. Fold in the raisins. Let the batter sit for 2 minutes before making the waffles; this allows the oatmeal to get moist and blend with the rest of the batter.

Make your waffles according to the manufacturer's directions, spraying or brushing the iron with oil between each waffle. Keep warm on a plate covered with foil until ready to serve.

PUMPKIN WAFFLES

MAKES TWELVE
6-INCH ROUND WAFFLES

2½ cups all-purpose flour

2½ teaspoons baking powder

½ teaspoon baking soda

½ teaspoon salt

2 teaspoons ground cinnamon

1 teaspoon ground ginger

½ teaspoon ground or freshly grated nutmeg

¼ teaspoon ground cloves

2 cups unsweetened almond milk

1 (15-ounce) can pureed pumpkin (not pumpkin pie mix)

⅓ cup canola oil

⅓ cup light brown sugar

2 teaspoons pure vanilla extract

I used to serve these at Sunday brunch at the Doghouse, a loft in Brooklyn I once lived in. It was so great to smell these cooking on those freezing-cold winter mornings. Yeah, we had no heat, but we compensated with the best vegan waffles you've ever tasted. Serve these with maple syrup and tempeh bacon. This recipe makes a lot of waffles, so feel free to halve it.

Preheat a waffle iron according to the manufacturer's instructions.

In a large mixing bowl, sift together the flour, baking powder, baking soda, salt, and spices. In a separate bowl, vigorously whisk together the milk, pumpkin, oil, brown sugar, and vanilla until well combined. Pour the wet ingredients into the dry and mix.

Make your waffles according to the manufacturer's directions, spraying or brushing the iron with oil between each waffle. Keep warm on a plate covered with foil until ready to serve.

MUFFINS
and SCONES

Whenever I bake muffins, I can't help but sing the Black Flag song "Rise Above." Then I get really vegan cheesy and change the lyrics around: "We are born with muffin pans! (Rise Above!) I am gonna have my pan (Rise Above!)." I can't believe I just told the world this, but try these delicious muffins and scones and that will help me save some face.

<<< THE BEST PUMPKIN MUFFINS, PAGE 45

½ cup raisins

1½ cups all-purpose flour

2 teaspoons baking powder

½ teaspoon baking soda

½ teaspoon ground cinnamon

¼ teaspoon ground or freshly grated nutmeg

¼ cup sugar

½ teaspoon salt

1 cup unsweetened almond milk (or preferred nondairy milk)

¼ cup canola oil

1 teaspoon pure vanilla extract

2 cups grated carrot

These are my favorite morning muffin. Since I weaned myself off of caffeine, I need a little kick to wake me up. Actually, I need several really hard kicks and in some cases a bucket of ice water dumped over my head. But what I'm saying is, once I'm awake the little bit of spice to these muffins seals the deal.

Preheat the oven to 400°F. Spray a 12-muffin tin with nonstick cooking spray or lightly grease with oil.

In a small bowl, soak the raisins in hot water to cover, set aside.

In a large mixing bowl, sift together the flour, baking powder, baking soda, cinnamon, nutmeg, sugar, and salt. Create a well in the center and add the milk, oil, and vanilla; mix with a wooden spoon until just combined. Fold in the grated carrots. Drain the raisins and fold in.

Fill each prepared muffin cup three-quarters full. Bake for 18 to 22 minutes, until a toothpick or knife inserted into the center of one comes out clean. When cool enough to handle, transfer to cooling racks to cool completely.

Fizzle says:

Soaking the raisins in hot water gives them new life and makes them plump and juicy. Just boil some water, put the raisins in a bowl, pour the water over them, and let them sit for a good 10 minutes.

CHERRY-ALMOND MUFFINS

MAKES 1 DOZEN MUFFINS

½ cup dried cherries, roughly chopped

2 cups all-purpose flour

⅓ cup sugar

2 teaspoons baking powder

½ teaspoon baking soda

¼ teaspoon salt

⅓ cup canola oil

¾ cup unsweetened almond milk (or preferred nondairy milk)

¾ cup plain vegan yogurt

2 teaspoons almond extract

1 cup sliced almonds

The cherry-almond combination is timeless. But one thing I didn't know ten years ago is that nobody, but nobody, has time to remove pits from cherries. I certainly don't anymore. So I've updated this recipe to use dried cherries like a normal person.

Preheat the oven to 400°F. Lightly grease a twelve-muffin tin.

In a small bowl, soak the cherries in hot water to plump them up. Set aside.

In a large bowl, sift together the flour, sugar, baking powder, baking soda, and salt. Create a well in the center and add the oil, milk, yogurt, and almond extract. Mix with a wooden spoon until combined. Fold in ¾ cup of the almonds; drain the cherries and fold them in, too.

Fill each prepared muffin cup three-quarters full; press the remaining sliced almonds into the tops of the muffins. Bake for 18 to 22 minutes, until a toothpick or knife inserted into the center of one comes out clean. When cool enough to handle, transfer to cooling racks to cool completely.

LEMON—POPPY SEED MUFFINS

MAKES 1 DOZEN MUFFINS

1¾ cups all-purpose flour

¼ cup sugar

1 tablespoon baking powder

¼ teaspoon salt

½ cup unsweetened almond milk (or preferred nondairy milk)

¾ cup plain vegan yogurt

⅓ cup canola oil

¼ cup freshly squeezed lemon juice

1 teaspoon pure vanilla extract

2 tablespoons finely grated lemon zest

1 tablespoon poppy seeds

This was one of the first recipes I made after creating the Post Punk Kitchen website and polling people on their favorite muffin. It really brings me back! I used to spend way too much time on the Internet, but at least it was producing muffins. These are plenty lemony with those fun crunchy pops of poppy. You don't wanna get everyone's favorite muffin wrong, and they seem to have stood the test of time, but I made them even a little more lemony for good measure.

Preheat the oven to 400°F. Spray a twelve-muffin tin with nonstick cooking spray.

In a large bowl, sift together the flour, sugar, baking powder, and salt. Create a well in the center and whisk in the milk, yogurt, oil, lemon juice, vanilla, and lemon zest. Fold the wet ingredients into the dry; halfway through mixing, fold in the poppy seeds.

Fill each prepared muffin cup two-thirds full. Bake for 20 to 25 minutes, until a toothpick inserted into the center comes out clean. When cool enough to handle, transfer to cooling racks to cool completely.

GINGER-RAISIN BRAN MUFFINS

½ cup raisins (see Fizzle says, page 38)

1½ cups all-purpose flour

2 teaspoons baking powder

½ teaspoon baking soda

½ cup sugar

2 teaspoons ground ginger

1 teaspoon ground cinnamon

½ teaspoon salt

¾ cup wheat bran

1¼ cups unsweetened almond milk (or preferred nondairy milk)

⅓ cup canola oil

1 teaspoon pure vanilla extract

¼ cup chopped crystallized ginger

I love the wheaty goodness of a bran muffin. These are elevated with ginger in both ground and crystallized form. I think bran gets a bad rap for being a health food, and people forget how yummy it is! This muffin will help them to remember.

Preheat the oven to 400°F. Lightly grease a twelve-muffin tin.

In a small bowl, soak the raisins in hot water to cover, set aside.

In a large mixing bowl, sift together the flour, baking powder, baking soda, sugar, ginger, cinnamon, and salt. Mix in the bran. Create a well in the center and add the milk, oil, and vanilla. Mix with a wooden spoon just until combined. Drain the raisins and fold them in along with the crystallized ginger.

Fill each prepared muffin cup most of the way full and bake for 20 to 22 minutes, until a toothpick or knife inserted into the center comes out clean. When cool enough to handle, transfer to cooling racks to cool completely.

SUNNY BLUEBERRY-CORN MUFFINS

1 cup all-purpose flour

1 cup finely ground cornmeal

1 tablespoon baking powder

½ teaspoon salt

⅓ cup sugar

¾ cup unsweetened almond milk (or preferred nondairy milk)

½ cup canola oil

2 tablespoons plain vegan yogurt

1 teaspoon pure vanilla extract

2 teaspoons lemon zest

1¼ cups blueberries

These are perfect sweet corn muffins, crispy outside and soft inside. They've got a great crumb, perfect for spreading with a pat of coconut oil. I call them sunny because of the lemon zest.

Preheat the oven to 400°F. Lightly grease a twelve-muffin tin.

In a large bowl, sift together the flour, cornmeal, baking powder, salt, and sugar. Create a well in the center and mix in milk, oil, yogurt, vanilla, and lemon zest. Fold in the blueberries, being careful not to overmix.

Fill each prepared muffin cup three-quarters full. Bake for 20 to 25 minutes, until a toothpick or knife inserted into the center of one comes out clean.

When cool enough to handle, transfer to cooling racks to cool completely, but they taste really good warm, too.

 *Fizzle says:*

To keep the blueberries from sinking to the bottom of the muffins, toss them around in a bowl of flour to coat. That will give them some "grip" in the batter.

THE BEST PUMPKIN MUFFINS

1¾ cups all-purpose flour

1 cup sugar

1 tablespoon baking powder

¼ teaspoon salt

1 teaspoon ground cinnamon

½ teaspoon ground or freshly grated nutmeg

½ teaspoon ground ginger

¼ teaspoon ground allspice

⅛ teaspoon ground cloves

1 cup pureed pumpkin
(fresh cooked or from a can;
do not use pumpkin pie mix)

½ cup unsweetened almond milk
(or preferred nondairy milk)

½ cup canola oil

2 tablespoons molasses

1 teaspoon pure vanilla extract

Everyone loves these muffins. (You think I throw around phrases like "the best" for nothing?) I created them when I was baking for a café and they sold like nobody's business. They truly are perfect in every way, and they fill your home with the most alluring autumnal scents. If I had to judge based solely on what muffins show up at every potluck I go to, I'd say these are definitely everyone's fave muffin from the book! I reduced the sugar a tiny bit from the original recipe, since that is what everyone seems to do with this recipe.

Preheat the oven to 400°F, and lightly grease a twelve-muffin tin.

Sift together the flour, sugar, baking powder, salt, and spices. Create a well in the center and mix in the pumpkin, milk, oil, molasses and vanilla, just until combined.

Fill each muffin cup two-thirds full. Bake for 18 to 20 minutes, until a toothpick or knife inserted into the center comes out clean. When cool enough to handle, transfer to cooling racks to cool completely.

VARIATION:

After mixing all the original ingredients, fold in a cup of either chopped fresh cranberries or chopped walnuts, or a mixture of the two.

MOCHA CHIP MUFFINS

1½ cups all-purpose flour

¾ cup sugar

¼ cup unsweetened cocoa powder

2½ teaspoons baking powder

½ teaspoon salt

2 teaspoons instant coffee powder

1 cup unsweetened almond milk
(or preferred nondairy milk)

½ cup canola oil

3 tablespoons plain vegan yogurt

1 teaspoon pure vanilla extract

½ cup vegan semisweet
chocolate chips

Here I go and break my own rule and make a muffin that is more like dessert. So, sue me. I use powdered instant coffee because I think its coffee flavor remains truer than that of freshly brewed coffee. If you don't have any instant coffee, just use an extra tablespoon of cocoa powder and have a chocolate–chocolate chip muffin.

Preheat the oven to 375°F. Lightly grease a twelve-muffin tin.

In a large bowl, sift together the flour, sugar, cocoa powder, baking powder, and salt. Mix in the instant coffee powder.

In a separate bowl, whisk together the milk, oil, yogurt, and vanilla.

Pour the wet ingredients into the dry and mix until the dry ingredients are moistened. Fold in the chocolate chips. Fill each prepared muffin cup three-quarters full. Bake for 18 to 20 minutes, or until a toothpick or knife inserted into the center of one comes out clean. When cool enough to handle, transfer to cooling racks to cool completely.

APPLE PIE–CRUMB CAKE MUFFINS

FOR THE TOPPING:

¼ cup all-purpose flour

¼ cup light brown sugar

½ teaspoon ground cinnamon

¼ teaspoon ground allspice

Pinch of salt

3 tablespoons canola oil

FOR THE MUFFINS:

1½ cups all-purpose flour

¼ cup plus 2 tablespoons granulated sugar

1 teaspoon baking powder

1 teaspoon baking soda

1 teaspoon ground cinnamon

½ teaspoon ground allspice

⅛ teaspoon ground cloves

¼ teaspoon salt

¾ cup apple juice or cider

⅓ cup canola oil

1 teaspoon pure vanilla extract

½ cup grated Granny Smith apple

½ cup chopped Granny Smith apple (¼-inch pieces)

The grated and chopped apples create an apple pie filling in the center of the muffin. It's a nice surprise to an already sweet and spicy treat. Crumbs, muffins, pie . . . what else could you ask for?

Prepare the topping by mixing all the dry topping ingredients together in a small bowl. Drizzle the oil in while mixing with your fingertips until crumbs form. Set aside.

Preheat the oven to 375°F, lightly grease a twelve-muffin tin.

In a large mixing bowl, sift together the flour, sugar, baking powder, baking soda, spices, and salt. Create a well in the center and add the apple juice, oil, and vanilla. Mix, then fold in the grated and chopped apple.

Fill each muffin cup two-thirds full. Sprinkle the crumb topping over each muffin. Bake for 22 minutes. When cool enough to handle, transfer to cooling racks to cool completely.

MARLENE'S GLAZED ORANGE SCONES

1¼ cups unsweetened almond milk
(or preferred nondairy milk)

1 tablespoon apple cider vinegar

3 cups all-purpose flour

⅓ cup sugar

2 tablespoons baking powder

¼ teaspoon salt

⅓ cup canola oil

3 tablespoons finely grated
orange zest

Orange Glaze (recipe follows)

I created this recipe specifically for my mom, who described to me the scone that she likes to get on her lunch hour at one of those overpriced French cafés in Union Square where she worked as a nurse. She still loves this recipe and makes it all the time! And she tells everyone the recipe was created for her. So, I've just gone ahead and added her name to the title.

Preheat the oven to 400°F. Lightly grease a cookie sheet.

In a measuring cup, combine the milk and vinegar, set aside to curdle.

In a large mixing bowl, sift together the flour, sugar, baking powder, and salt. Add the milk mixture, oil, and orange zest and mix until just combined; the dough should be clumpy and not sticky. Even if there is still a light dusting of flour, that's okay.

Divide the dough in two. Knead one portion a few times, then form into a 6-inch disk. Cut the disk into six slices (pizza style), and place each slice on the prepared cookie sheet. Do the same with the remaining dough. Bake for 12 to 15 minutes, until slightly browned on the bottom and firm on top. Transfer to a cooling rack.

When cool (if they are still only slightly warm, that is okay), transfer to parchment paper. Pour about 2 tablespoons Orange Glaze over each scone; let the tops set before eating. If you simply can't wait, prepare to have sticky fingers.

ORANGE GLAZE

1 cup confectioners' sugar

2 tablespoons refined coconut oil,
melted

2 tablespoons fresh orange juice

1 teaspoon finely grated orange zest

Sift the confectioners' sugar into a mixing bowl; add all the other ingredients and mix until smooth.

SCONES

1 cup plus 2 tablespoons
unsweetened almond milk
(or preferred nondairy milk)

2 teaspoons apple cider vinegar

3 cups all-purpose flour

2 tablespoons baking powder

¼ cup sugar, plus an extra teaspoon
for sprinkling the tops

¼ teaspoon salt

¼ cup refined coconut oil

¼ cup canola oil

Scones are not just flat muffins, as some cafés would have you believe; they're more like doughy biscuits that are sweet but not overly so. I've updated this recipe a little bit, mostly to make the ingredients more accessible, but also because in the past decade I've learned the joys of coconut oil and I just can't make scones without it these days. It makes them so buttery and almost like a shortbread. Perfecto.

This is the basic recipe, but really, who makes plain old scones with nothing in 'em? Use one of the variations below and enjoy teatime in style.

Preheat the oven to 400°F. Lightly grease a cookie sheet.

In a measuring cup, stir together the milk and vinegar. Set aside to curdle.

In a large mixing bowl, sift together the flour, baking powder, sugar, and salt. Add the coconut oil in teaspoonfuls and cut it into the flour with a pastry cutter or your fingers. Add the milk mixture and canola oil. Mix until just combined; the dough should be clumpy and not sticky. Even if there is still a light dusting of flour, that's okay.

Drop by ¼ cupfuls onto the prepared cookie sheet and pat the tops just a bit to round them out; sprinkle with a bit of sugar. Bake for 12 to 15 minutes, until slightly browned on the bottom and firm on the top.

CONTINUED >>>

VARIATIONS:

Add these ingredients to the batter after mixing all the original ingredients:

BERRY SCONES: Fold in 1½ cups of blueberries, raspberries, or blackberries.

BERRY-LAVENDER SCONES: In addition to the berries, add 1 tablespoon of chopped, dried food-grade lavender.

CHOCOLATE CHIP SCONES: Add 1 teaspoon of pure vanilla extract to the liquid ingredients, add 2 tablespoons of sugar, and fold in 1 cup of vegan chocolate chips.

CHOCO-GINGER SCONES: Add ½ cup of finely chopped crystallized ginger along with the chocolate chip variation.

MAPLE WALNUT SCONES: Add 2 teaspoons of maple extract to the liquid ingredients, add 2 tablespoons of sugar, and fold in 1½ cups of walnuts.

HAZELNUT SCONES

½ cup unsweetened almond milk (or preferred nondairy milk)

2 teaspoons apple cider vinegar

⅓ cup refined coconut oil

¼ cup sugar, plus an extra teaspoon for sprinkling on the tops (optional)

3 cups all-purpose flour

2 tablespoons baking powder

¼ teaspoon salt

½ teaspoon freshly grated nutmeg

¾ cup freshly brewed hazelnut coffee, cooled

1 teaspoon pure vanilla extract

½ cup toasted and coarsely chopped hazelnuts (see Fizzle says)

 *Fizzle says:*

Toast the hazelnuts on a baking sheet at 350°F for about 12 minutes, tossing occasionally. Wrap the nuts in a kitchen towel for 2 minutes while they are still warm, then rub the nuts together so that any burnt skins come off. Chop carefully on a cutting board so that they don't roll all over the place, or use a food processor fit with a metal blade to chop them.

Ground hazelnuts give these scones a rich texture. A touch of freshly brewed hazelnut coffee elevates them to hazelnut heaven, and the chopped hazelnuts are the icing on the cake (or the hazelnuts on the scone, as the case may be). The scones taste great still warm, topped with coconut oil and apple butter. I recommend brewing a whole pot of the hazelnut coffee and cooling the rest to have iced hazelnut coffee alongside your scones.

Preheat the oven to 400°F. Lightly grease a cookie sheet.

In a measuring cup, stir together the milk and vinegar. Set aside to curdle.

In a large bowl, cream together the coconut oil and sugar.

In a large mixing bowl, sift together the flour, baking powder, and salt. Mix in the nutmeg. Add the shortening mixture in clumps (use a teaspoon or your fingers) and mix with your fingertips or a pastry knife until the mixture resembles coarse crumbs. Add the milk mixture, coffee, and vanilla and mix with a wooden spoon until just combined; fold in the chopped hazelnuts. The dough should be clumpy and dry; even if there is still a light dusting of flour, that's okay.

Drop by ¼ cupfuls onto the prepared cookie sheet; sprinkle with a little sugar if you like. Bake for 12 to 15 minutes, until slightly browned on the bottom and firm on the top.

SOUPS

I love making soup for several reasons, like it's delicious and fast, but the biggest impetus is that everything goes in one pot and there aren't a gazillion dishes to clean up (or let sit in the sink for a week) afterward. The delicious aromas don't hurt, either. All of these soup recipes are hearty enough to be meals, with some rice or good crusty bread. Sometimes I double these recipes and make a big batch to either freeze or eat throughout the week. You can freeze soup in airtight freezer bags for up to a month. Okay, maybe I sometimes let them go a little longer than that.

◀◀◀ CHILI SIN CARNE AL MOLE, PAGE 68

3 pounds carrots, peeled and diced into a little smaller than ½-inch pieces

1 large yellow onion, chopped

2 tablespoons olive oil

2 cloves garlic, minced

1 tablespoon minced fresh ginger

1 tablespoon mild curry powder

½ teaspoon salt

A few dashes of freshly ground black pepper

3 cups vegan vegetable broth

1 (13-ounce) can coconut milk

1 tablespoon pure maple syrup

I've never been crazy about carrot soups; they always seemed a little too skimpy and health-foody for me. But this slightly sweet, incredibly creamy, and hearty carrot soup changed all that. It's easy to make, to boot. It's really easy to fancy up, too. Swirl in some coconut milk, top with a few pepitas and microgreens, and you've got a ten-dollar bowl of soup!

Heat a 4-quart pan over medium heat. Cook the carrots and onion in the olive oil for 7 to 10 minutes; cover and cook, stirring occasionally, until the onion is lightly browned. Add the garlic, ginger, curry, salt, and pepper; sauté for 1 more minute. Add the broth, cover, and bring to a boil. Lower the heat and simmer for 10 to 12 minutes, or until the carrots are tender.

Add the coconut milk and bring to a low boil. Turn off the heat. Use an immersion blender to puree half of the soup; if you don't have one, then puree half of the soup in a blender and add it back to the soup pot (see Fizzle says). Add the maple syrup and stir. Serve hot.

 *Fizzle says:*

If you are using a blender to puree the soup, let the soup cool a bit so that the steam doesn't cause the blender lid to pop off and splatter hot soup everywhere. Once the soup has cooled enough, give it a few pulses in the blender, lift the lid to let steam escape, and repeat.

CHIPOTLE, CORN, AND BLACK BEAN STEW

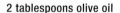

SERVES 6

2 tablespoons olive oil

1 large onion, quartered and thinly sliced

3 cloves garlic, minced

2 teaspoons ground cumin

½ teaspoons salt

A few dashes of freshly ground black pepper

4 chipotle peppers (canned), seeded and chopped (see Fizzle says, page 62)

1 (28-ounce) can crushed tomatoes

3 cups vegan vegetable broth

4 Yukon gold potatoes, cut into ¾-inch dice

2 large carrots, peeled, cut into ¾-inch dice

1 cup corn kernels (if using fresh, it's 2 ears)

1½ cups cooked black beans (or 1 [15-ounce] can, drained and rinsed)

½ cup chopped fresh cilantro

2 tablespoons freshly squeezed lime juice

I still make a version of this stew a few times a month. It's spicy and hearty and smoky and so so so flavorful. And it's one of those recipes that you can really mess around with; add zucchini or cauliflower or whatever vegetables you have around. You can also try different beans; pintos or chickpeas are nice choices.

Heat a 4-quart pan over medium heat. Sauté the onion in the olive oil for about 5 minutes, until translucent. Add the garlic, cumin, salt, and black pepper. Sauté for 1 minute more. Add the chipotles, tomatoes, broth, potatoes, and carrots, cover, bring to a low boil, and simmer for 20 minutes.

Uncover and add the corn and beans. Thin with a little water, if needed. Cook, uncovered, for 5 more minutes. Add the cilantro and lime juice. Let sit for at least 10 minutes. Serve.

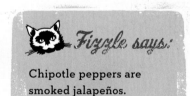

Fizzle says:

Chipotle peppers are smoked jalapeños.

1 tablespoon olive oil

1 medium-size yellow onion, diced medium

1 large red bell pepper, diced small

1 cup carrot, peeled and cut into ½-inch dice

2 jalapeño peppers, seeded and thinly sliced (use just one if you like less heat) (see Fizzle says, page 62)

1 teaspoon dried rosemary

1 teaspoon dried thyme

A few dashes of freshly ground black pepper

1 teaspoon salt

3 cups vegan vegetable broth

3 cups fresh corn kernels (from about 5 ears of corn)

2 medium-size russet potatoes, peeled and sliced into ½-inch chunks

1 bay leaf

Pinch of cayenne pepper

2 tablespoons freshly squeezed lime juice

1 tablespoon pure maple syrup

OPTIONAL GARNISHES:

Sliced radishes

Chives

You don't need cream in this chowder; potatoes give this soup a creamy, hearty body. All the fresh ingredients really let the pure corn flavor shine and the jalapeños give it just a little kick.

Heat a 4-quart pan over medium heat. Sauté the onion, bell peppers, carrot, and jalapeños in the olive oil with a pinch of salt until the onion is translucent, about 7 minutes. Add the rosemary, thyme, black pepper, and salt; sauté for 1 minute more. Add the broth, corn, potatoes, bay leaf, and cayenne. Cover and bring to a boil, then lower the heat and simmer for 20 minutes, or until the potatoes are tender. Uncover and simmer for 10 minutes more to let the liquid reduce a bit.

Remove the bay leaf and puree half of the chowder either using an immersion blender or by transferring half of the chowder to a blender, pureeing until smooth (see Fizzle says, page 56), and adding back to soup. Add the lime juice and maple syrup to taste, thin with a little water if it seems too thick, and simmer for 5 more minutes. Let sit for at least 10 minutes and serve.

Fizzle says:

Fresh corn is really the way to go here. But frozen will work, too!

BEET, BARLEY, AND BLACK SOYBEAN SOUP WITH PUMPERNICKEL CROUTONS

2 tablespoons olive oil

1 large yellow onion, diced medium

3 cloves garlic, minced

2 teaspoons dried tarragon

A few dashes of freshly ground black pepper

8 cups vegan vegetable broth

4 medium-size beets, peeled, cut in half, sliced ¼ inch thick (about 4 cups)

¾ cup pearl barley

¼ cup tamari or soy sauce

1 (15-ounce) can black soybeans, drained and rinsed (about 2 cups)

2 tablespoons balsamic vinegar

½ cup chopped fresh dill

Pumpernickel Croutons (recipe follows)

We created a soup like this for Food Not Bombs, in San Francisco, and I will always remember how happy it made everyone (except for my roommate who was pissed at me for dumping a whole bottle of her tamari into the soup. She was also pissed at me for not paying rent, but that's another matter entirely). Eating this soup makes me think I am in Mother Russia in the late nineteenth century; I've come home after strolling the promenade in Saint Petersburg and I'm getting ready to complete the next chapter of my tragic novel, but first—soup.

Heat a 4-quart pan over medium heat. Sauté the onion in the olive oil with a pinch of salt for 5 minutes, until translucent. Add the garlic, tarragon, and pepper; sauté until fragrant (about a minute). Add the broth, beets, barley, and tamari, cover, and bring to a boil. Lower the heat and simmer for 30 minutes. Add the beans and simmer for another 10 to 15 minutes, stirring frequently to prevent the barley from sticking together, or until the barley is tender. Add the balsamic vinegar and fresh dill. Serve with Pumpernickel Croutons, and garnish with more fresh dill.

PUMPERNICKEL CROUTONS

2 tablespoons olive oil

½ teaspoon dried tarragon

¼ teaspoon salt

4 slices firm pumpernickel bread, cut into ¼-inch dice

Preheat the oven to 400°F.

In a wide, shallow bowl, stir together the olive oil, tarragon, and salt. Add the diced bread and toss gently to coat. Spread the bread in a single layer on a cookie sheet; toast for 8 to 10 minutes, stirring once. Remove from the oven and let cool.

5 pounds butternut squash (about 3), bulbous part cut from the stem part, then each part sliced in half, seeds removed

4 tablespoons olive oil

1 medium-size yellow onion, diced medium

1 serrano chile, chopped and seeded

1 tablespoon minced fresh ginger

3 cloves garlic, minced

1 teaspoon salt

4 cups vegan vegetable broth

1 tablespoon pure maple syrup

2 tablespoons freshly squeezed lime juice

This is such a fresh, simple way to eat autumn. Roasted squash needs very little to make it shine; a touch of spice, some ginger, and you're getting one big cozy fall hug in a bowl. You can use a jalapeño instead of a serrano if you'd like a little less heat.

Preheat the oven to 425°F.

Lightly grease a rimmed baking sheet with cooking spray or brush lightly with oil. Place the squash, cut side down, on the baking sheet and wrap the sheet with foil. Bake for 40 to 45 minutes, or until the squash is tender and easily pierced with a fork.

When the squash is about 15 minutes from being done, preheat a stockpot over medium heat. Sauté the onion in the olive oil for 5 minutes, with a pinch of salt, until translucent. Add the chiles; sauté for 5 minutes more. Lastly, add the ginger, garlic, and salt; sauté for 2 minutes more.

When the squash is ready, scoop the yummy squash meat out of the skin and transfer to the pot. Add the broth, maple syrup, and lime and puree with an immersion blender. Let sit for 10 minutes for the flavors to marry, then taste for salt and serve!

 Fizzle says:

Be very careful when working with hot peppers, the white lining in the pepper contains a chemical called capsaicin, which gives the pepper its heat. Don't ever touch the inside of the pepper with your bare hands or they will burn for hours and sometimes even the next day (if you touch your eyes, you'll feel like you were just maced by the police at a Critical Mass demo). Either work very carefully with a small paring knife or employ a pair of disposable gloves while cutting and chopping.

CURRIED SPLIT PEA SOUP

1 tablespoon olive oil

1 medium-size yellow onion, diced small

3 cloves garlic, minced

2 tablespoons minced fresh ginger

2 teaspoons curry powder

1 teaspoon ground cumin

¼ teaspoon ground coriander

¼ teaspoon ground cardamom

A generous pinch of ground cinnamon

2 teaspoons salt

8 cups vegan vegetable broth

1 pound dried split peas

1 medium-size carrot

Fresh cilantro for garnish (optional)

You've got to have a split pea soup simmering on the stovetop at least a few times a month during the winter. This one, laced with curry flavors, might be a little change up for your split pea routine. Serve it as an entrée with some jasmine rice or as the perfect starter to an Indian meal. You will be surprised and relieved at how easy it is to prepare.

In a stockpot, sauté the onion in the olive oil over medium heat for about 5 minutes. Add the garlic, ginger, spices, and salt. Sauté for 2 more minutes.

Add the broth and stir well. Add the split peas. Cover and bring to a boil.

Bring the heat back down to medium, then simmer for about an hour, until the peas are tender. Grate in the carrot and serve. You can garnish with fresh cilantro, if you have it on hand.

POTATO-ASPARAGUS SOUP

3 pounds Yukon gold potatoes, cut into 1-inch chunks

1 pound asparagus, rough ends discarded, tips cut into 2-inch pieces, lower part cut into ½-inch pieces

2 tablespoons olive oil

1 large yellow onion, diced medium

3 cloves garlic, minced

1 teaspoon salt

A few dashes of freshly ground black pepper

4 cups vegan vegetable broth

2 bay leaves

2 tablespoons freshly squeezed lemon juice

¼ cup chopped fresh dill

I didn't spice this up too much because asparagus is my favorite spring vegetable and I like its fresh flavor to shine through. Lemon and dill bring out the gardeny aromas. If you like a chunkier soup, then just puree half of the soup, or use an immersion blender to puree to your liking.

Place the potatoes in a stockpot and cover with cold water. Cover the pot and bring to a boil, then lower the heat and simmer for 20 minutes, or until tender. Add the asparagus, boil for 3 minutes, drain, and set aside.

Rinse out the pot, then in the same pot, sauté the onion in the olive oil for 5 to 7 minutes; add the garlic, salt, and black pepper; and sauté for 2 more minutes. Add the broth and bay leaves, boil for 10 minutes, then discard the bay leaves. Add the potatoes and asparagus, heat through, then puree three quarters of the soup in a blender or food processor (see Fizzle says, page 56). Add a squeeze of lemon and serve garnished with fresh dill.

BLACK BEAN AND QUINOA SOUP

1 tablespoon olive oil

1 yellow onion, diced medium

4 cloves garlic, minced

1 cup chopped fresh tomato

1 teaspoon ground cumin

½ teaspoon dried oregano

½ teaspoon crushed red pepper flakes

½ cup uncooked quinoa

1 large carrot, cut into ¼-inch pieces

2 bay leaves

4 cups vegan vegetable broth

1 (24-ounce) can black beans, liquid reserved

½ cup chopped fresh cilantro, plus extra for garnish

FOR SERVING:

A few handfuls of tortilla chips

2 avocados

Fizzle says:

Black beans, especially the canned ones, tend to be salty, so there's no specific quantity of salt here. Definitely salt to taste!

The thing about this soup is that it's almost the only time ever when I don't rinse the canned beans. The whole shebang is poured right in, creating a flavorful, full-bodied broth that is so monumentally satisfying with the chewy quinoa. Of course, for seasoning, we have our usual black bean soup suspects—cumin, oregano, bay, cilantro—and all that flavor just gets sealed into the delicious broth. It's familiar but definitely not ordinary.

Heat a 4-quart pot over medium heat. Sauté the onion in the olive oil with a pinch of salt, for about 5 minutes, until translucent. Add the garlic and sauté with the onion for a few seconds. Then add the chopped tomato, cumin, oregano, and red pepper flakes and cook for a minute or so, just to break down the tomatoes a bit.

Add the quinoa, carrot, and bay leaves, and then pour in 2 cups of the broth. Cover and bring to a boil. Let boil for 5 minutes or so, until the veggies are al dente (that's mostly tender with a little bite).

Add the remainder of the broth, the black beans with their liquid, and the cilantro. Cover and bring to a boil, then remove the lid, lower the heat to a simmer, and cook for 10 more minutes or so, to cook the quinoa the rest of the way.

Taste for salt and seasonings; adjust if you like. Turn off the heat and let sit for 10 minutes or so to allow the flavors to marry. Remove the bay leaves and serve topped with crushed tortilla chips, avocado, and cilantro.

CHILI SIN CARNE AL MOLE

⅓ cup olive oil

1 large onion, chopped

1 small jalapeño pepper, minced
(see Fizzle says, page 62)

1 small red bell pepper, chopped

3 cloves garlic, smashed

1 pound seitan, coarsely chopped
into ¼-inch cubes

2 tablespoons chile powder

1 teaspoon ground cinnamon

½ teaspoon ground cumin

1 (28-ounce) can whole, peeled
tomatoes in sauce

3 tablespoons unsweetened
cocoa powder

3 tablespoons blackstrap molasses

2 (14-ounce) cans pinto beans,
drained and well rinsed

2½ cups vegan vegetable broth

This is Terry Hope Romero's recipe and I am a better woman for having made it about a million times by now. The chocolate gives the chili a traditional mole flavor that is otherworldly. Terry tells us, "I like thick, chunky bean and vegetable-filled vegetarian chili as much as the next guy, but I've always had a longing for a meatless version of the more traditional Mexican-style chili con carne—a dark red broth, large chunks of meat, accompanied only by a few bits of onions, chiles, and spices. Seitan is ideal for this recipe, but being a meatless version it would seem rather stark without the addition of good old pinto beans. The consistency is more like a very chunky, thick soup than your usual stewlike chili. Like most soups and stews, this chili tastes even better reheated the next day."

Heat a 6-quart pot over medium-high heat. Sauté the onion and peppers in oil for 2 minutes, then add the garlic and seitan. Cook for 8 minutes, until the onion is soft. Add the chile powder, cinnamon, and cumin, and cook, stirring constantly, for another minute. Add the tomatoes, cocoa powder, and molasses. Stir and break up the tomatoes with the back of a spoon, then add the beans and broth. Cover and bring to a gentle boil, then lower the heat and simmer for about 30 minutes. Allow to sit at least 20 minutes before serving.

CHICKPEA AND RICE SOUP WITH A LITTLE KALE

¾ cup cashews, soaked in water for 2 hours or overnight (see Fizzle says, page 117)

2 tablespoons olive oil

1 medium-size yellow onion, thinly sliced

3 cloves garlic, minced

1 teaspoon dried rosemary

¾ teaspoon dried thyme

1 teaspoon salt

Freshly ground black pepper

¾ cup uncooked rice, rinsed (see Fizzle says)

3 ribs celery, thinly sliced

1 cup carrot, diced chunky

5 cups vegan vegetable broth

1 (24-ounce) can chickpeas, drained and rinsed (about 3 cups)

4 cups chopped kale

Thinly sliced green onion, for garnish

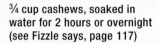 *Fizzle says:*

Red rice is cool here, but you can use whatever kind you like. Maybe basmati, maybe wild rice. Just note that brown rice will have a longer cooking time, so plan accordingly.

Invite a friend over, break some bread (olive sourdough spoken here), and inhale big bowlfuls of comfort like this one: chewy rice and succulent chickpeas, fragranced with rosemary, thyme, and celery, pulled together by luscious cashew cream. And, of course, I throw in a little kale at the end for good measure. Lacinato holds its bite, but you can use whatever kale tickles your fancy.

Drain the cashews and place them in a blender or food processor with 1 cup of fresh water. Blend until completely smooth, scraping the sides with a spatula occasionally to make sure you get everything. This could take 1 to 5 minutes, depending on the strength of your blender.

Heat a stockpot over medium heat. Sauté the onion in the olive oil, with a pinch of salt, for about 5 minutes, until translucent. Add the garlic, rosemary, thyme, salt, and pepper and sauté for a minute more.

Add the rice, celery, and carrot and then pour in the broth. Cover and bring to a boil. Once boiling, bring the heat down to a simmer, add the chickpeas, and let cook for about 15 more minutes, until the rice is cooked and the carrot is tender.

Add the cashew cream and kale and simmer until the kale is wilted, 3 to 5 more minutes. You may need to add water to thin the soup if it seems too thick. Taste for salt and seasonings and let sit for 10 minutes or so to allow the flavors to marry. Serve topped with green onions.

This soup thickens as it cools, so if you have leftovers, just thin with a little water when you reheat.

1½ cups matzoh meal

¾ teaspoon salt, plus extra for the boiling water

¾ teaspoon freshly ground black pepper

1 (12-ounce) package firm silken tofu, such as Mori-nu (the vacuum-packed kind)

8½ cups or so Rich Vegetable Broth (page 75)

¼ cup plus 2 tablespoons extra-virgin olive oil

1 medium-size carrot, peeled

A handful of fresh dill, coarsely chopped

Fresh parsley for garnish

Nothing speaks to a Brooklyn Jewish girl's heart more than a matzoh ball. These are perfect light, fluffy, and flavorful matzoh dumplings. Use homemade vegetable stock to add tons of love and flavor. I suggest making the Vegetable Broth (page 75) the night before. You can even make the matzoh mixture the night before, and the big day will be a breeze.

If you don't have a huge stockpot (I use a 16-quart), then halve the recipe or boil the matzoh balls in two sessions. I make my own matzoh meal by grinding the matzoh in a food processor (it takes about six sheets to get the 1½ cups called for in this recipe) but store-bought will work just as well.

In a mixing bowl, combine the matzoh meal with the salt and pepper; set aside.

Crumble the tofu into a blender or food processor, add ½ cup of the broth, and puree until smooth. Add the oil and blend again.

Mix the tofu mixture with the matzoh meal, making sure that everything is moist. Grate half of the carrot into the mixture and mix until it's well distributed. Cover the bowl with plastic wrap and refrigerate for at least an hour and up to overnight. You can't skip this step; it's important in making sure that the matzoh balls will not fall apart when boiled.

When you are ready to form the balls, fill a large stockpot with enough water to fit all the matzoh balls with minimal touching. Salt the water generously, cover, and bring to a low boil.

Set out a cutting board upon which to line up the formed matzoh balls, and cover it with parchment paper, if you have any, to prevent sticking. Also have handy a wet rag to wipe your hands on between forming each matzoh ball.

Remove the matzoh mixture from the fridge. Form into tightly packed, walnut-size balls and place on the prepared cutting board. When all the balls are prepared, drop carefully into the boiling water, one or two at a time,

with a spatula or slotted spoon. It should be just above a simmer, not a roaring boil, or the balls will fall apart. Take your time and be careful not to plop one on top of another; they need to remain separate. When all the balls are in the water, cover the pot and DO NOT LIFT LID FOR 40 MINUTES! Sorry for the caps, just had to stress it. When the 40 minutes are up, you can remove the lid. The matzoh balls will have floated to the top and will drop back down when lid is lifted. This is fun to watch.

Now they are ready to serve; however, to make them even lighter, you can turn off the heat, cover the pot again, and let them sit in the water for another hour or so. This way they absorb more water and expand a bit more.

Prepare the remaining 8 cups of broth by placing it in a separate pot. Grate the other half of the carrot into the broth, along with adding a healthy handful of fresh dill. Bring to a low boil, and when it's just heated, you're ready to prepare the bowls.

With a slotted spoon, carefully remove the matzoh balls from their pot and place two or three in each bowl. Ladle the broth over the matzoh balls, so that they're covered only about halfway. You can garnish with some more fresh dill, or parsley. Serve to whomever you love.

If you are not serving the soup right away, you can refrigerate the matzoh balls overnight, and boil them when ready to prepare the soup. Some people even freeze leftovers, but I never have as there've never been leftovers.

WHITE BEAN AND ROASTED GARLIC SOUP

2 tablespoons olive oil

1 medium-size yellow onion, diced medium

1 teaspoon salt

A few dashes of freshly ground black pepper

½ teaspoon whole fennel seeds, crushed (see Fizzle says, page 17)

4 cups vegan vegetable broth

3 cups cooked great northern beans (or 2 [15-ounce] cans, drained and rinsed)

3 fresh sage leaves, finely chopped

1 bay leaf

2 heads garlic, roasted (see Fizzle says)

1 tablespoon freshly squeezed lemon juice

Serve this creamy soup with garlic croutons or a nice crusty bread. When you eat this soup, you will be transported to a rustic villa in Italy where the air is clean and fresh, the locals are provincial but friendly, and you have the solitude you need to finish your sonnets. If you have never roasted garlic before, you don't know what you are missing; it adds a great depth of flavor. I like to think of it as a "restaurant taste," for lack of a better phrase. You can garnish with a few fresh herbs, if you like, or even just a simple spray of freshly ground black pepper.

Heat a 4-quart pan over medium heat. Sauté the onion in the olive oil for about 5 minutes, until translucent.

Add the salt, black pepper, and fennel seeds; sauté for 1 minute. Add the broth, beans, sage, and bay leaf, bring to a boil, then lower the heat and simmer, uncovered, for 5 minutes.

Remove the bay leaf. Add the roasted garlic and use an immersion blender to puree. Or puree in batches in a standing blender or food processor (see Fizzle says, page 56). Return the mixture to the pot and add the lemon juice. Taste for salt and serve!

 Fizzle says:

TO ROAST GARLIC: Preheat the oven to 350°F. Peel off as much of the papery skin as you can and put the garlic in the oven for about 30 minutes. Remove from the oven and, when cool, squeeze out the garlic or peel away the skin from each clove.

RICH VEGETABLE BROTH

1 tablespoon olive oil

1 large onion, skin included, coarsely chopped

2 large carrots, peeled and coarsely chopped

2 parsnips, peeled and coarsely chopped

3 cloves garlic, smashed

2 leeks, well rinsed and coarsely chopped

1 cup loosely packed fresh parsley

1 cup loosely packed fresh dill

1 teaspoon salt

I make this broth to use with my matzoh ball soup. You can use other veggies, such as celery, squash, potatoes, or mushrooms; just make sure there is enough water to cover everything. Keep the skins on the onions for added color and flavor. You can also try other herbs, such as thyme, rosemary, bay leaves, and peppercorns, for a stronger broth.

Heat a 6-quart stockpot over medium heat. Sauté the onion in the olive oil for about 5 minutes on medium heat. Add all the other ingredients and 9 cups of water and bring to a boil. Lower the heat and let simmer for 1½ hours, uncovered.

Let the broth cool until it's an okay temperature to handle. Strain into a large bowl through cheesecloth or a very fine-mesh strainer. Press the vegetables with a gentle but firm pressure to get all the moisture out.

This will keep in the fridge in a tightly sealed container for up to 3 days, or freeze for up to 3 months.

LITTLE MEALS, FINGER FOODS, and SAMMICHES

These little meals and finger foods can be considered appetizers, snacks, or in some cases hors d'oeuvres. They are all great things to bring to a potluck or to serve when you have friends over for board game night. And the sammiches, well, they're sammiches! Great for lunch or dinner.

<<< SPANAKOPITA, PAGE 95

FRESH CORN FRITTERS

6 ounces extra-firm silken tofu (½ package of the vacuum-packed kind)

1 tablespoon pure maple syrup

2 tablespoons unsweetened almond milk (or preferred nondairy milk)

¼ cup all-purpose flour

3 ears corn, kernels cut from the cob (see Fizzle says) (about 1½ cups)

¼ teaspoon salt

A few dashes of freshly ground black pepper

1 jalapeño pepper, seeded and very finely chopped (see Fizzle says, page 62)

¼ cup red bell pepper, very finely chopped

Refined coconut oil for frying

These are really fast and yummy. The jalapeño and red pepper make the pancakes colorful and add just a little spice. Serve with salsa or as a breakfast side dish in place of potatoes. A cast-iron skillet works best for even frying.

In a blender or food processor, whiz the tofu, maple syrup, milk, and flour, scraping down the sides often with a rubber spatula, until everything is smooth. Add half of the corn (¾ cup) and pulse so that the mixture is blended but still a bit chunky. Transfer to a bowl and add the remaining corn, salt, black pepper, jalapeño, and bell pepper, and combine well.

Heat a thin layer of oil in a heavy skillet over medium-high heat. Drop the batter by tablespoonfuls into the skillet. Flatten a little with the back of the spoon (wet the spoon first to avoid sticking). Cook in batches, 2½ to 3 minutes on each side, until lightly browned. When done, transfer to a brown paper bag or paper towels to drain the oil.

Fizzle says:

To cut the corn from the cob, place the shucked corn pointy side up on a kitchen or paper towel. Take a chef's knife and cut downward, as close as you can to the cob. The towel will keep the corn kernels from bouncing everywhere and also makes a handy vehicle for transporting them to the mixing bowl.

FOR THE KNISHES:

7 medium-size russet potatoes

4 medium-size sweet potatoes (about 2 pounds)

FOR THE DOUGH:

2 tablespoons olive oil, plus extra for brushing

¾ cup cold water

1 teaspoon salt

1 teaspoon baking powder

3 cups all-purpose flour

FOR THE FILLINGS:

1 large yellow onion, finely chopped (about 2 cups)

4 tablespoons olive oil

1 teaspoon salt

¼ teaspoon freshly ground black pepper

1 (10-ounce) package frozen spinach, thawed and drained (drain while potatoes bake)

¼ teaspoon ground or freshly grated nutmeg

¼ teaspoon ground cinnamon

¼ teaspoon ground ginger

Knishes, if you don't know, are like the Jewish empanada: a stuffed dough filled with fabulous stuff, most traditionally potato. I like to make all three fillings at once because it's easy enough to do and the colors look really cool together. The real work here is the dough, which you have to knead for a long time to get it smooth and stretchy enough; after that you are halfway to knish madness. There are a lot of steps but actually not so much active prep/cooking time, so don't be intimidated.

BAKE THE POTATOES:

Preheat the oven to 350°F. Prick the seven regular potatoes with a fork and wrap in foil and place in the oven. The four sweet potatoes can just go in as is. Take out the sweet potatoes after 40 minutes; the regular potatoes will need to bake for another 30 minutes, so they will take about 70 minutes total, depending on their size. Remove from the oven and let cool. Once the potatoes are cool enough to handle, remove the skins with a peeler or paring knife.

TO MAKE THE DOUGH:

By hand: In a large bowl, place one peeled, baked russet potato; let the others continue to cool. Add the oil and ¾ cup cold water to the potato and mash until well combined. Add the salt and baking powder, and then add the flour in batches, kneading with each addition. Knead until you have a smooth dough. This can take up to 15 minutes by hand, so have someone nearby to help knead in case your little hands get tired. Let the dough rest while you prepare the fillings.

Using a mixer: In the work bowl of a standing mixer fitted with a dough hook, place one peeled potato and mash it up a bit with the oil and ¾ cup cold water. Add the salt and baking powder, and then add the flour in batches, mixing after each addition. Let knead until a smooth dough forms, about 15 minutes. Let the dough rest while you prepare the fillings.

CONTINUED >>>

FOR THE POTATO KNISHES:

In a medium-size skillet, sauté the onion in 2 tablespoons of the olive oil over medium heat for 15 minutes, until browned and slightly caramelized.

Mash the remaining six peeled, baked russet potatoes in a large bowl. Add the cooked onion, the remaining 2 tablespoons of olive oil, and salt and pepper to taste. Mash together well. Reserve half of the mashed potato filling in a separate bowl for the spinach filling.

FOR THE SPINACH KNISHES:

Add the thawed, drained spinach to reserved half of the mashed potato filling and mix until well combined.

FOR THE SWEET POTATO KNISHES:

Mash the baked sweet potatoes. Add the ginger, nutmeg, cinnamon, and salt, and mix well.

TO ASSEMBLE AND BAKE THE KNISHES:

Preheat the oven to 350°F.

Cut the dough into three equal portions. Roll out one portion as thinly as possible, into a 14 x 6-inch rectangle. Sprinkle with flour as you roll, to keep the dough unsticky.

Place 2½ cups of a single filling down the center of the rolled-out portion of dough. Spread out so that the filling is roughly 12 x 2 inches. Fold the dough over the filling the long way to create a roll. Trim the ends of the roll-up to where the filling begins. Place, folded side down, on a lightly greased baking sheet.

Repeat with the other two portions of dough and the other two fillings. (You may have extra filling, depending on how big your potatoes were. Don't overstuff the knishes; just bite the bullet and eat the filling on its own.)

With a knife, score each roll into fifths. That will give them a nice shape and make them easier to cut when they are done. Brush each lightly with olive oil. Bake for 40 minutes.

Remove from the oven; let cool just enough so that you can slice them. Serve warm, with plenty of mustard for the potato and spinach ones.

OLIVE, TOMATO, AND MILLET—STUFFED ZUCCHINI

SERVES 8

1 medium-size yellow onion, finely chopped

1 tablespoon olive oil

2 cloves garlic, minced

½ cup millet, rinsed

½ teaspoon dried rosemary

½ teaspoon dried thyme

½ teaspoon dried marjoram

½ teaspoon dried basil

1 teaspoon paprika

A few dashes of freshly ground black pepper

½ teaspoon salt

1 (28-ounce) can whole tomatoes with juice

2 cups vegan vegetable broth or water

4 medium-size zucchini, ends trimmed

½ cup chopped, pitted kalamata olives

¼ cup capers

Chopped fresh parsley for garnish

Zucchini boats are perfect vehicles for transporting the tangy olive-tomato-millet combination into your mouth. Millet was an under-represented grain ten years ago . . . and it still is today! It must be looking at quinoa with envy and exasperation. But let millet into your life. It's got a nutty flavor, it cooks up quick and it's about one-quarter the price of quinoa.

In a 4-quart saucepan, sauté the onion in the olive oil over medium heat for 5 to 7 minutes, until the onion is translucent. Add the garlic and sauté until fragrant, about a minute.

Add the millet, herbs, spices, and salt; sauté for about 3 minutes. Add the tomatoes, crushing them with your hands as you add them. Add the tomato juice and broth. Cover the pot and bring to a boil, then lower the heat and simmer with the lid ajar for 20 minutes.

Meanwhile, prepare the zucchini: Slice in half lengthwise. Place, cut side down, in a large saucepan, then fill the pan with enough water to cover the zucchini halfway. Cover the pan, bring to a boil, then cook for 5 minutes. Remove the zucchini from the water and place on a plate to cool. Once cool enough to handle, use a tablespoon to remove their pulp, leaving only about ¼ inch of pulp in the zucchini. Chop the removed pulp and reserve.

Preheat the oven to 350°F.

Add the zucchini pulp, olives, and capers to the millet mixture. Simmer for about 5 more minutes, until the millet is tender.

Stuff each zucchini half with some of the mixture. Place in a baking dish and bake for about 20 minutes. Let cool for about 5 minutes and garnish with parsley before serving.

POTATO SAMOSAS WITH COCONUT-MINT CHUTNEY

MAKES 36 SMALL SAMOSAS
OR 18 LARGE ONES

FOR THE DOUGH:

¾ cup unsweetened almond milk
(or preferred nondairy milk)

¼ cup olive oil

1 tablespoon apple cider vinegar

About 3 cups all-purpose flour

¼ teaspoon ground turmeric

¼ teaspoon baking powder

1 teaspoon salt

FOR THE FILLING:

3 medium-size russet potatoes,
peeled and cut into 1-inch chunks

2 tablespoons olive oil, plus extra
for brushing

1 teaspoon whole cumin seeds

2 teaspoons whole mustard seeds

1 medium-size yellow onion,
very finely chopped

1 cup finely diced carrot

2 cloves garlic, minced

1 tablespoon minced fresh ginger

1 teaspoon ground coriander

½ teaspoon ground turmeric

Pinch of cayenne pepper

1 teaspoon salt

1 tablespoon freshly squeezed
lemon juice

¾ cup frozen peas

Samosas are crispy pockets of dough stuffed with a rich and flavorful filling. I can't imagine starting any Indian meal without them. Most New Yorkers are familiar with the strip of Indian restaurants on 6th Street that try to lure you in with Christmas lights and promises of the best samosas, but all too often these samosas are an oily mess that have been sitting under a heat lamp for far too long. The samosas I make are baked, not fried, and just as crisp and heavenly as deep-fried ones. Serve with Coconut-Mint Chutney (recipe follows).

In a 4-quart pot, submerge the potatoes in water. Cover and bring to a boil, and then lower the heat to simmer for about 10 more minutes, until fork tender. When they are ready, drain and set aside.

Preheat the oven to 400°F.

TO MAKE THE DOUGH:

While the oven preheats, pour the wet dough ingredients into a large mixing bowl. Add 2 cups of the flour, and mix in the turmeric, baking powder, and salt. Begin kneading the mixture, adding the rest of the flour gradually until a smooth not sticky dough is formed, about 10 minutes.

Set the dough aside, cover with a wet cloth or wrap in plastic wrap, and begin preparing the filling.

TO PREPARE THE FILLING:

Heat a large skillet over medium-low heat. Add the olive oil, cumin seeds, and mustard seeds. The seeds will begin to pop. You may want to employ a lid to keep from getting hit with any popping seeds. Let them pop for about a minute, then add the onion and carrot. Raise the heat to medium-high and sauté for 7 to 10 minutes, until the onion begins to brown. Add the garlic, ginger, coriander, turmeric, cayenne, salt, and lemon juice, and sauté for a minute more. Add the potatoes, mashing with a potato masher as you go along. When potatoes are mashed well and heated through, fold in the peas.

TO ASSEMBLE:

Divide the dough in half and roll one portion out on a floured surface, about ⅛ inch thick (so, rather thinly.) Now comes the fun part (or the pain in the ass, depending on your temperament). Let's form the little cutie pies. Have a small bowl of water ready. With a 4-inch cookie cutter (or something with a 4-inch circumference), cut out eight circles.

FOR SMALL COCKTAIL SAMOSAS:

Cut the dough circles in half, creating semicircles. Gently pull the dough to stretch it a bit. With your fingertips, brush the cut edge with water, then fold it over, corner to corner, and seal along the straight edge with your thumb and forefinger. You should now have a cone. Stuff 1½ to 2 teaspoons of filling into the cone, then dab the open edges with water and again seal with your fingers. Repeat until you have thirty-six samosas.

FOR REGULAR-SIZE SAMOSAS:

Instead of slicing the dough circles in half, place 1½ tablespoons of filling in the center of an entire circle, then dab the circumference with water, fold over the filling to form a pillowy semicircle, and seal with your thumb and forefinger.

TO BAKE:

Brush each side of the samosas lightly with oil and place on a baking sheet that has been sprayed with nonstick cooking spray or very lightly brushed with oil. For large samosas: Bake for 15 minutes; flip the samosas over

Fizzle says:

To make frozen peas taste like peas and not like freezer, run them under cool water to remove the icy freezer stuff, then drain.

and bake for 10 more minutes, or until lightly browned. For small samosas: Bake for 12 minutes; flip over and bake for 8 minutes, or until lightly browned. I like to let them sit for at least 5 minutes to let the crust flake just right. These freeze well; to reheat, bake small ones at 350°F for 20 minutes, larger ones for 25 to 30 minutes.

COCONUT–MINT CHUTNEY

½ cup coconut milk

⅓ cup finely chopped fresh mint

⅓ cup finely chopped fresh coriander

1 clove garlic, minced

1 teaspoon agave nectar

1 tablespoon freshly squeezed lime juice

¼ teaspoon salt

Mix together all the ingredients in a medium-size bowl and refrigerate for an hour or so, to let flavors meld. Bring to room temperature to serve.

BLACK BEAN, MUSHROOM, AND QUINOA—STUFFED PEPPERS

2 tablespoons olive oil,
plus extra for baking

1 medium-size yellow onion,
diced small

3 cloves garlic, minced

2 cups finely chopped cremini
mushrooms

1 tablespoon mild chile powder

1 teaspoon salt

½ cup uncooked quinoa

1 (15-ounce) can tomato sauce

4 large red bell peppers

1½ cups cooked black beans
(or 1 [15-ounce] can, drained
and rinsed)

1 teaspoon pure maple syrup

Fresh cilantro for garnish

Again, this is a recipe inspired by my mom. She had been making stuffed peppers for years from a recipe off a veggie crumbles package. She bugged me pretty much daily to put that recipe in the cookbook and I had to remind her, "Mom, no prepackaged foods, for the love of God!" One day she came over armed with the recipe and was determined to somehow force it into the cookbook. We came up with this recipe instead, and now everyone is happy.

Heat a 4-quart pot over medium heat. Sauté the onion in the oil for 3 to 5 minutes, until translucent. Add the garlic and mushrooms; sauté for about 5 minutes, until the mushrooms have released their moisture. Stir in the chile powder and salt. Add the quinoa and 1 cup of the tomato sauce (reserve the rest) along with ¼ cup of water, lower the heat and cover, and simmer for about 20 minutes, stirring once.

Meanwhile, preheat the oven to 350°F and prepare the peppers. Cut the tops off the peppers and remove the seeds. Lightly coat with olive oil, sprinkle with salt, and place upside down in a baking dish. Parbake for about 10 minutes, just to soften, then remove from the oven, but don't turn the oven off.

When the quinoa filling is cooked, stir in the beans and maple syrup. Use a spoon to stuff each pepper with filling and stand them upright in the baking dish. Pour the remaining tomato sauce over the peppers and bake for 15 minutes. Remove from the oven, garnish with cilantro, and serve.

FRESH MANGO SUMMER ROLLS WITH SWEET AND SPICY DIPPING SAUCE

MAKES 25 ROLLS

4 ounces very thin rice noodles

25 rice paper wrappers
(plus extra in case some tear)

¼ cup roasted peanuts,
very finely chopped

1 mango, peeled and sliced
into matchsticks (see Fizzle says,
page 167)

1 ripe avocado, peeled and
cut into long, thin slices

1 cup bean sprouts (or seedless
cucumber, sliced into matchsticks)

½ cup fresh cilantro leaves

Sweet and Spicy Dipping Sauce
(page 90)

Crisp vegetables and sweet mango make these the perfect treat for a hot summer's night when the last thing you want to do is turn on the oven. The avocado provides the perfect creaminess to make them complete. The noodles are the only things that require cooking, and they're done in 10 minutes.

Cook the noodles according to the package directions. Drain and run them under cold water until they feel cool. Transfer them to a bowl and begin your rolls.

Have ready a pie pan or large, wide bowl filled with hot water (tap water is fine) and clean counter space or a cutting board. Place the rice paper wrappers, two at a time, into the water until they are flexible (30 seconds to a minute). Carefully remove from water and lay flat on a clean surface. In the lower two-thirds of the roll, place a tablespoon of noodles and sprinkle a few of the chopped peanuts (about ½ teaspoon) over them. On top of that, place four mango strips and a slice or two of avocado. On top of that, place six or seven bean sprouts and three or four cilantro leaves. Fold the left and right sides over the filling, then take the bottom of the wrapper and begin rolling. It may take a couple of tries to get it right, but keep it up and you're on your way to summer roll heaven. Keep wrapped and chilled until ready to eat and serve with small finger-bowls of the dipping sauce.

CONTINUED >>>

>>> CONTINUED FROM PREVIOUS PAGE

 *Fizzle says:*

A great way to keep summer rolls fresh if you aren't serving immediately is to line a baking dish with damp paper towels. Then line the rolls in a single layer. Add another layer of damp towels, and another layer of rolls. Finally, cover with more damp paper towels, wrap in plastic wrap, and refrigerate. They will keep for up to a day. If you are choosing to do this, then remember to sprinkle the avocado with lemon juice before rolling, so that it stays fresh and green.

SWEET AND SPICY DIPPING SAUCE

MAKES ¾ CUP

¼ cup rice vinegar

1 tablespoon sriracha

1 teaspoon toasted sesame oil

1 garlic clove, minced

3 tablespoons roasted peanuts, chopped

1½ teaspoons sugar

In a small bowl, vigorously mix all the ingredients together with ¼ cup of water and chill until ready to serve. Serve in tiny dipping bowls.

SEITAN AND HERB–STUFFED MUSHROOMS

MAKES 30 LARGE MUSHROOMS

30 large white mushrooms (about 1½ pounds), wiped clean

½ cup seitan, diced as small as you can make it

3 tablespoons olive oil

1 small onion, very finely chopped (1 cup)

2 cloves garlic, minced

¼ teaspoon dried thyme

¼ teaspoon dried basil

¼ teaspoon dried oregano

½ teaspoon salt

A few dashes of freshly ground black pepper

¼ cup chopped fresh parsley

1 teaspoon finely grated lemon zest

2 tablespoons freshly squeezed lemon juice

¾ cup plain vegan bread crumbs

⅓ cup shelled walnuts

These make great hors d'oeuvres or appetizers for an Italian meal. They are very omnivore-friendly, so don't hesitate to serve them to your Uncle Ted who still thinks that passing you turkey at Thanksgiving is the funniest joke ever.

Preheat the oven to 375°F.

Remove the stems from the mushrooms. Chop them and set aside to be used in stuffing.

Heat a large pan over medium-high heat. Sauté the stems and seitan in the olive oil for about 5 minutes. Add the onion, garlic, dried herbs, and salt and pepper, and sauté for 5 more minutes. Add the parsley, lemon zest, and lemon juice, and mix well. Cook for 3 more minutes. In a large bowl, combine the vegetable mixture, bread crumbs, and walnuts. Use your hands to mix well. If the mixture is too dry, add water by the tablespoonful until the mixture holds together when pinched.

Lightly grease a large rimmed baking sheet with olive oil and sprinkle with a little salt. The salt goes a long way to making sure the mushrooms aren't bland.

Spoon the filling into the mushrooms so that it rises above the rim about ¾ inch. Transfer mushrooms to the baking sheet and drizzle each with a little olive oil. Bake for 20 to 25 minutes; the mushrooms should be tender and browned. Serve warm or at room temperature.

 *Fizzle says:*

Try to find mushrooms that are at least 1½ inches in diameter, so that you have plenty of space for the stuffin'!

BLACK-EYED PEA AND QUINOA CROQUETTES WITH MUSHROOM SAUCE

1½ cups cooked black-eyed peas, drained (or 1 [15-ounce] can, drained and rinsed)

1 tablespoon olive oil

1 tablespoon soy sauce

1 cup cooked quinoa, at room temperature

½ teaspoon dried thyme, crumbled

½ teaspoon dried basil, crumbled

1 teaspoon smoked paprika

FOR THE BREAD CRUMB COATING:

½ cup vegan bread crumbs

⅛ teaspoon salt

A few dashes of freshly ground black pepper

½ teaspoon finely grated lemon zest

2 teaspoons olive oil

All too often quinoa is made into a salad or thrown willy-nilly under a stir-fry. Hey, I'm guilty there, too. But I wanted to give it the royal treatment in the form of these cute, savory croquettes. I love the crunchy texture and super-savory flavor. If you'd like this to be more of an entrée, some Garlicky Kale (page 128) would do the trick.

Preheat the oven to 350°F.

In a mixing bowl, mash the black-eyed peas with a potato masher. Add the olive oil and soy sauce and stir. Add the quinoa, herbs, and paprika and combine the mixture with your hands. Refrigerate for 30 minutes. You should be able to mold the mixture into balls that readily stick together.

In a small bowl, mix together all the ingredients for the breading. Spray a baking pan with a little oil. Form the croquettes into walnut-size balls. Gently roll the balls between your palms three or four times, then flatten out into a thick disk. Toss each disk with the bread crumbs to coat, and place on the prepared baking sheet. When all the croquettes have been formed, spray lightly with oil. Bake for 40 minutes, turning once after 20 minutes.

I serve these by putting some cooked quinoa into the center of the plate, then putting four croquettes around the quinoa, then putting a healthy dose of mushroom sauce on the quinoa. Don't pour the sauce directly on the croquettes or they will get mushy.

MUSHROOM SAUCE

3 cups vegan vegetable broth

2 tablespoons organic cornstarch

1 tablespoon olive oil

1 small onion, finely chopped

2 cloves garlic, minced

2 cups cremini mushrooms, thinly sliced

1 teaspoon dried thyme

1 teaspoon salt

A few dashes of freshly ground black pepper

½ cup dry white wine

3 tablespoons soy sauce

¼ cup nutritional yeast flakes

¼ cup unsweetened almond milk (or preferred nondairy milk)

Yes, this sauce will make your croquettes sing (in that food-singing sort of way). But don't stop at croquettes. This makes a great sauce for pasta, gravy for mashed potatoes, and poured on absolutely everything during Thanksgiving. Or just grab and spoon and eat it straight up.

In a small bowl, whisk the cornstarch into the broth until dissolved. Set aside.

In a medium-size saucepan, sauté the onion and garlic in the olive oil for 3 minutes. Add the mushrooms, thyme, salt, and pepper and cook for 5 minutes, stirring occasionally. Add the white wine and turn the heat up to high to bring to a boil for 3 minutes.

Add the soy sauce and the broth mixture, stirring to make sure no clumps form. Bring to a boil and then lower the heat and simmer for 15 minutes, stirring occasionally. Add the nutritional yeast and whisk until dissolved. Add the milk and whisk for another minute or so. Let cool for a few minutes before serving.

SPANAKOPITA
(SPINACH PIES)

YIELD VARIES DEPENDING ON SHAPE (SEE BELOW)

¼ cup plus 2 tablespoons olive oil, plus extra for brushing the phyllo

2 bunches fresh spinach, rinsed very well, long stems removed

1 bunch scallions, trimmed and finely chopped

3 cloves garlic, minced

1 cup chopped fresh dill

2 pounds firm tofu, drained and pressed

⅓ cup freshly squeezed lemon juice

2 teaspoons dried oregano

Dash of ground or freshly grated nutmeg

¾ cup finely ground walnuts

¼ cup nutritional yeast

1 teaspoon salt

Several dashes of freshly ground black pepper

1 (1-pound) box frozen phyllo dough, thawed overnight

My friend Terry Hope Romero brings us this awesome recipe that I have enjoyed at many a potluck. She offers us three different ways to make it: a simple triangle shape, a wacky spiral, and a layered pie in a casserole dish. The tangy, herby filling is perfect in the flaky phyllo dough.

Heat a large, heavy-bottomed pan over medium heat. Sauté the spinach, scallions, garlic, and dill in 2 tablespoons of the olive oil until the spinach is completely wilted. Add the spinach in small batches if the pot is too full. Cook for about 7 minutes. Remove from the heat and set aside to cool to room temperature.

In a large bowl, mash the drained tofu (use your hands for more control) to a ricotta-like consistency. Take the cooled spinach mixture by small handfuls and squeeze out as much liquid as humanly possible (discard the liquid); add the squeezed spinach to the tofu. Add the lemon juice, oregano, nutmeg, ground walnuts, ¼ cup of the olive oil, and the nutritional yeast. Mix well with your hands; season with salt and pepper. Taste the mixture; it should taste pleasantly salty and tangy. Make sure the filling has cooled to room temperature before stuffing into the phyllo dough as directed.

TRADITIONAL TRIANGLE SHAPE:
MAKES ABOUT 30 TRIANGLES

Preheat the oven to 350°F. Take two sheets of dough; brushing olive oil generously onto one sheet, layer the second sheet on top, also brushing that sheet with oil. Score the stacked dough sheets lengthwise into three strips. With the short end of a strip nearest you, place a scant 2 tablespoons of filling toward the top left corner of the long rectangle. Grabbing the corner of the dough, fold it rightward so it forms a triangle, fold it toward the left to form another triangle, and continue folding in this manner (like folding a flag, try burning this . . .) until you just can't fold any more. Wrap any remaining bit of dough around, underneath the triangle. Brush with lots of olive oil and bake on a baking sheet for 10 to 12 minutes, until deep golden brown and puffy. These can burn easily, so watch it!

CONTINUED >>>

BACK-TO-ATHENS COIL SHAPE:

MAKES ABOUT 15 ROUND SPANAKOPITA

Terry says: "I have no idea if Socrates would teach at the foot of a mountain of these back in ancient Greece . . . just that all the spanakopita I ate in Greece were shaped like these. They are basically cute snail-shaped buns. They never get as brown as the triangles and are a little less flaky but still yum."

Preheat the oven to 375°F. Taking two sheets, brush with oil as for the triangles. Score the dough lengthwise into two strips. Run 2 to 3 tablespoons of filling along one long edge of each piece. Carefully roll up the long strip, starting from the filling side, to form a long, thick rope o' spanakopita. Then, daintily roll up your coil to form a snail-shaped bun. Brush with lots of oil. Bake for about 25 minutes, until golden brown on top and lightly browned on the bottom.

EASY AS π SHAPE:

SERVES 8

You have no time for horrible Greek jokes so this one's for you: a spinach pie casserole, neat square slices well suited for serving as an entrée with salad.

Preheat the oven to 375°F. Prepare eight sheets of dough with olive oil as for the triangle shape. Oil a 9 x 12- to 13-inch baking dish and, place the dough layers inside, patting any extra dough up the sides of the pan. Gently spread the spinach mixture on top of the dough. Prepare another eight layers of phyllo (or add a few more layers if you have leftover dough), put on top of the spinach layer, and tuck into the sides of the pan any overhanging dough.

Lightly score the top layer of dough into eight rectangles of equal size (this will prevent the dough from crumbling too much when slicing after it's baked). Brush with lots of olive oil. Bake for 35 to 40 minutes, until golden brown, being careful not to let the phyllo burn.

Fizzle says:

Phyllo is full of surprises the first time you handle it. You can't expose it to air for more than a few seconds before it dries out and becomes completely useless, so have handy several damp, clean kitchen towels and some plastic wrap. Don't spaz out! It's easy once you get the hang of it, and you'll be making phyllo this and that all the time and soon your friends will have to plan some kind of intervention. To make your life easier, make sure you have plenty of workspace on a clean, smooth surface. Since you'll be working with olive oil, have handy one of those pump mist sprayers that you can fill with any oil of choice. Or just have a bowl filled with olive oil and apply with a pastry brush.

PARSNIP-SCALLION PANCAKES

MAKES ABOUT
16 PANCAKES

4 cups shredded, peeled parsnip

1 cup finely chopped scallions

½ cup all-purpose flour

2 teaspoons canola oil,
plus extra for frying

½ teaspoon salt

A few dashes of freshly
ground black pepper

Parsnips: the other white vegetable. They're more than just a pale carrot. They're fresh and earthy tasting with just a hint of sweetness that doesn't need too much spicing up. The green onions add just enough subtle bite.

Combine the parsnip and scallions in a large mixing bowl, mixing to evenly distribute the scallion. Add the flour, oil, salt, and pepper, tossing to coat. Add ⅓ cup of water and mix until the batter holds together when given a squeeze. Add a little more water, if necessary.

Heat a large, heavy-bottomed skillet over medium-high heat. Add about ¼ inch of oil. To test whether the pan is ready, throw in a little pinch of the batter; if bubbles form around it immediately, the pan is hot enough. Form about 2 tablespoons of batter into a ball, then flatten out into a disk about 2 inches wide. Add the pancake to the oil, and continue with the rest of the batter, without crowding, cooking each pancake for 2½ to 3 minutes on each side, until golden brown. Note: I usually make a batch of eight; by the time the eighth is placed in the pan, the first pancake that I put in is ready to be flipped. You may need to add extra oil when you make the second batch.

When the pancakes are done, transfer to a paper bag to drain the oil. Then serve!

CAULIFLOWER-LEEK KUGEL
with ALMOND-HERB CRUST

SERVES 8 TO 12

6 cups cauliflower florets

3 sheets of matzoh

1 (12-ounce) package extra-firm silken tofu

4 tablespoons olive oil

4 cups coarsely chopped leeks (white and light green parts only), well rinsed

1 small yellow onion, cut into ½-inch dice

½ cup chopped fresh parsley

½ cup chopped fresh dill

1½ teaspoons salt

½ teaspoon freshly ground black pepper

½ cup almonds, toasted and chopped

I was making this with my mom one Passover and she kept exclaiming how wonderful the dill smells and how I should be grateful that the Absolute has provided such an abundance of fresh leafy things. Then she went on and on about how I should join her philosophy school so I could learn to appreciate things. Then she asked me why I don't get laser surgery to remove my tattoos. You see, in Jewish culture, even something as simple as a great-smelling herb can lead to nagging. Fortunately she only had yums and mmms while we were eating. This recipe was inspired by one in *Bon Appétit* magazine, veganized, modified, and vastly improved. If you eat tofu on Passover, then it's Passover happy.

Preheat the oven to 350°F.

Bring to boil a large pot of water. Add the cauliflower and cook for 10 minutes, covered.

Meanwhile, crumble two sheets of matzoh into a food processor or blender. Grind the matzoh into crumbs; remove from the food processor and set aside. Crumble the tofu into the food processor or blender, and puree until smooth. You may have to add a couple of tablespoons of water to make it completely smooth. Set aside until ready to use.

When the cauliflower is done, drain and transfer to a large bowl. Mash coarsely with a potato masher.

Heat 2 tablespoons of the olive oil in a large skillet over medium-high heat. Add the leeks and onion; sauté until the leeks are tender and the onion is translucent, about 5 minutes. Add to the cauliflower. Mix in the matzoh crumbs. Add the pureed tofu, 1 tablespoon of the parsley, 1 tablespoon of the dill, salt, and pepper, and mix well.

Brush or spray a 9 x 13-inch casserole dish with oil. Spread the cauliflower mixture evenly in the dish.

Now make the topping. In a medium-size mixing bowl, mix together the almonds and remaining herbs. Crumble the remaining matzoh into large crumbs with your fingers and add to the almond mixture. Drizzle in the remaining 2 tablespoons of olive oil and mix. Sprinkle this mixture evenly over the kugel.

Bake for 35 minutes, until browned on top. Remove from the oven and let cool for at least 30 minutes before digging in.

Fizzle says:

Kugel **officially means "pudding" in Yiddish, but in reality it describes any casserole.**

CHICKPEA-BROCCOLI CASSEROLE

SERVES 6 TO 8 AS A SIDE DISH

3 (16-ounce) cans chickpeas, drained and rinsed (or 5 cups cooked chickpeas)

1 large onion, quartered and thinly sliced

3 large carrots, grated (about 2 cups)

1 head broccoli, cut into small florets (about 4 cups)

2 tablespoons thinly sliced chives (optional)

½ cup vegan bread crumbs (preferably whole wheat)

3 tablespoons olive oil

1 cup vegan vegetable broth

1 teaspoon salt

VARIATION:

SPICED-UP CHICKPEA-BROCCOLI CASSEROLE:
Add 1 teaspoon of dried thyme, 2 teaspoons of onion powder, freshly ground black pepper to taste, and a pinch of red pepper flakes along with the bread crumbs.

This is a nice healthy veggie-ful meal, especially if you're feeling lazy, since all the ingredients go into one pan. After the prep work, you bake it for an hour while you kick back and pay the bills or update your blog. Sometimes you just want the comforting taste of veggies without all those pesky spices, but I've added a spiced-up version for when you're in the mood.

Preheat the oven to 350°F.

In a large bowl, mash the chickpeas well, using a potato masher or a firm fork; it takes about 2 minutes to get the right consistency. Add the vegetables and mix well. Add the bread crumbs and mix, then add the oil and mix again. Finally, add the broth and salt, and mix one last time. Transfer all ingredients to a 9 x 13-inch (preferably glass or ceramic) casserole dish. Press the mixture firmly into the casserole. Cover with foil; bake for 45 minutes. Uncover and bake for 15 more minutes. Serve it hot the day of, but it tastes good cold as well.

FALAFEL

2 cups cooked chickpeas

½ cup vegan bread crumbs

¼ cup chickpea flour

1 medium-size onion,
finely chopped

2 cloves garlic, chopped

½ teaspoon baking powder

1 teaspoon ground cumin

1 teaspoon ground coriander

¼ teaspoon cayenne pepper

¼ cup finely chopped fresh
flat-leaf parsley

½ teaspoon salt

A few dashes of freshly
ground black pepper

Vegetable oil for frying

FOR SERVING:

4 large pita breads, sliced in half
to make 2 pockets apiece

Lettuce

Chopped tomato, red onion,
and cucumber

Tahini Dressing (page 130)

If you attended Jewish day camp, you might have grown up think-
ing that Judaism was a series of humiliating acts wherein you had
to don curious things on your head and wear brightly colored face
paint and then dance around in the hot sun while lethargic adults looked
on. Case in point: One summer, my fellow campers and I dressed up
as falafel and sang a song to the tune of the Kinks' "Come Dancing." It
went "Fa-la-fel . . . I like to eat it on a Saturday; fa-la-fel . . . the taste is
natural." Somehow I came out of all this still loving falafel to pieces. If
you don't have a food processor, you can still make it by chopping the
onion, garlic, and parsley as finely as possible and then mashing everything really, really, really well.

In a food processor, combine the chickpeas and bread crumbs; pulse for about 30 seconds until the chickpeas are chopped. Add the remaining ingredients (through the black pepper) and process, scraping down the sides, until relatively smooth but somewhat coarse. The mixture should look fairly green from the parsley. Transfer to a bowl, cover, and refrigerate for at least 30 minutes.

Shape the batter into 1½-inch balls and then flatten into 2-inch-diameter patties. In a large, heavy-bottomed pan (cast iron is ideal), heat about ½ inch of vegetable oil. Test the oil by throwing in a pinch of the batter; if the oil immediately bubbles up rapidly, it is ready. Cook the patties in the oil in two batches, 2½ to 3 minutes per side. Remove with a slotted spoon and transfer to a flattened paper bag or paper towels to drain.

Prepare the sammiches by stuffing the pita bread with falafel, lettuce, tomato, red onion, and cucumber, and drizzling in the tahini dressing.

CURRIED TEMPEH–MANGO SALAD SAMMICHES

MAKES 4 SAMMICHES

1 (8-ounce) package tempeh

1 tablespoon soy sauce

1 cup mango (less than 1 mango), peeled and chopped into ¼-inch chunks (see Fizzle says, page 167)

¼ cup chopped scallions

FOR THE DRESSING:

3 tablespoons vegan mayo

2 teaspoons curry powder

¼ cup freshly squeezed lime juice

1 teaspoon sugar

1 teaspoon sriracha

Pinch of salt

FOR SAMMICHES:

2 large pita breads, sliced in half to make 2 pockets apiece

Lettuce

Thinly sliced red onion

Extra mango slices

I usually make a sandwich out of these but the salad would be just as good over some greens. Mangoes and tempeh are surprisingly compatible, and the curry powder pulls everything together.

Tear the tempeh into bite-size pieces and place in a small saucepan. Cover with water and add the soy sauce. Cover the pot and bring to a boil, then simmer for 15 minutes. Drain and transfer the tempeh to a bowl to cool.

Meanwhile, whisk together all the ingredients for the dressing.

Add the mango and scallions to the tempeh. Add the dressing; mix well. Cover and refrigerate for at least an hour and up to overnight, to allow flavors to meld. Adjust the seasonings as you see fit. Serve in pitas with lettuce, red onion, and extra mango slices.

LENTIL-WALNUT BURGERS

1 teaspoon to 2 tablespoons olive oil, to taste

1 small yellow onion, diced medium

½ pound cremini mushrooms, thinly sliced

3 cloves garlic, minced

Freshly ground black pepper

½ teaspoon dried thyme

½ teaspoon fennel seeds, crushed (see Fizzle says, page 17)

1 (15-ounce) can lentils, drained and rinsed (or 1¼ cups cooked)

2 tablespoons soy sauce or tamari

2 teaspoons freshly squeezed lemon juice

¼ teaspoon liquid smoke (optional)

1 cup vegan bread crumbs

½ cup chopped walnuts

Cooking spray

These burgers are hearty and toothsome and perfectly sturdy . . . everything you want in a veggie burger! Serve them diner-style, on a nice fluffy bun with ketchup (and mayo for me), pickles, tomato, and lettuce, and add a little avocado, if you like. I also like to use these burgers to top salads covered in Tahini Dressing (page 130). They turn out great when baked but if you'd like to fry them, be my guest!

Preheat the oven to 350°F.

Heat a large, heavy-bottomed, non-stick pan (preferably cast iron) over medium-high heat. Sauté the onion in the oil for about 3 minutes with a pinch of salt. Add the mushrooms, garlic, black pepper, thyme, and fennel and sauté for 7 to 10 minutes, until the mushrooms are cooked.

When the mushrooms have cooked, transfer the mushroom mixture to a food processor. Add the lentils, soy sauce, lemon juice, and liquid smoke, if using. Add ½ cup of the bread crumbs, reserving the other ½ cup. Pulse until mostly smooth, but there should still be a little texture. Transfer to a large mixing bowl. Add the remaining ½ cup of bread crumbs to the burger mixture, along with the chopped walnuts, and thoroughly combine.

Divide the burger mixture into six equal pieces. An easy way to do this is divide it in half, then cut each half into three basically equal portions. You can do that right in the bowl if it's large enough.

Line a baking sheet with parchment paper and spray with cooking spray. Form the mixture into patties, spray with a little more cooking spray, and bake for 15 minutes. Flip the burgers and bake for 12 to 15 more minutes, until nicely browned.

They taste great served immediately but they're also excellent at room temperature, so don't be afraid to stuff into a sandwich and take as a lunch.

TEMPEH REUBEN

FOR THE MARINATED TEMPEH:

½ cup white cooking wine

2 tablespoons olive oil

2 tablespoons balsamic vinegar

2 tablespoons tamari

2 tablespoons freshly squeezed lemon juice

2 cloves garlic, smashed

1 pound tempeh, cut widthwise into four equal pieces, then cut through the middle so that you have eight thin rectangles

FOR THE DRESSING:

⅓ cup vegan mayo

2 tablespoons ketchup

2 tablespoons freshly squeezed lemon juice

1 tablespoon minced onion

3 teaspoons capers

2 tablespoons sweet pickle relish (or equivalent amount chopped pickles)

A pinch of cayenne pepper

FOR ASSEMBLY:

8 slices good, dark pumpernickel bread

4 teaspoons olive oil

If I haven't told you enough times, I was practically raised in a Jewish deli. I especially loved big Reubens filled with plenty of sauerkraut, Thousand Island dressing, and the nontraditional pickle. I do get a little misty eyed when I pass a deli and can't pay a visit to my lost love Reuben, but sometimes he is waiting for me at home.

Marinate the tempeh: Combine all the ingredients for the marinade, except the tempeh. Add the tempeh and marinate for at least an hour, turning once.

Meanwhile, mix together all the dressing ingredients and set aside.

When the tempeh has marinated for an hour, preheat a grill pan over high heat. Cook the slices on the grill for 4 minutes on one side, until dark grill lines have appeared, then use tongs to flip them over and cook on the other side for about 3 minutes.

To prepare the sammiches, brush one side of each slice of bread lightly with olive oil. Heat a large skillet over medium heat. Fry each piece of bread on the oiled side for 3 minutes, flip over, and cook for 1 minute more (it's okay that the other side is dry).

Divide the sammich ingredients equally among four oiled-side-down fried bread slices. Smother in dressing, top each serving with another slice of fried bread, nonoiled side down, cut in half, and serve. For that authentic Jewish deli look, stick a toothpick in each half.

 *Fizzle says:*

You can get canned, jarred, or bagged sauerkraut at the grocery store, but for the best results ask the deli counter at your supermarket if it has any fresh sauerkraut.

TLT
(TEMPEH, LETTUCE, AND TOMATO)

MAKES 4 SAMMICHES

8 slices sourdough bread, toasted

1 cup hummus

1 batch Tempeh Bacon (page 19)

1 large tomato, thinly sliced

Thinly sliced red onion

4 leaves romaine lettuce

1 cup alfalfa sprouts

Smoky tempeh bacon and hummus (and lettuce and tomato)—absolutely delish. I love the hippie addition of alfalfa sprouts, but I'm vegan, so go figure.

Layer one slice of bread with hummus; pile on the tempeh bacon, then the tomato, onion, lettuce, and sprouts. Add a dollop of hummus to keep the sammich intact, top with another slice of bread, slice in half, and serve. Repeat for the other three sammiches.

CHICKPEA-NORI SALAD SAMMICHES

MAKES 4 SAMMICHES

1 (15-ounce) can chickpeas, drained and rinsed

3 tablespoons vegan mayo

2 tablespoons apple cider vinegar

2 tablespoons minced onion

½ cup peeled, shredded carrot

1 tablespoon finely chopped nori

Salt and freshly ground black pepper

8 slices whole wheat bread, toasted

Sammich fixings (lettuce, tomato, and onion)

Okay, you got me: I miss tuna fish sandwiches. These sammiches satisfy my craving, using nori for a hint of the sea. If you've had sushi before, you're already acquainted with nori, only here we are chopping it up and treating it more like a spice.

In a large bowl, mash the chickpeas with a potato masher until no whole beans are left. Add the remaining ingredients (through the pepper) and mix well. Serve on toasted whole wheat with lettuce, tomato, and onion.

 *Fizzle says:*

Chickpeas act so much like tuna salad in this recipe that I always come running when I hear the can open! You will need about one-quarter sheet of nori to get the table-spoon called for in this recipe.

TOFU-DILL SALAD SAMMICHES

14 ounces extra-firm tofu, drained and pressed

3 tablespoons minced red onion

3 tablespoons vegan mayo, plus extra for serving

1/3 cup fresh dill, chopped

2 teaspoons Dijon mustard

2 tablespoons freshly squeezed lemon juice

Salt and freshly ground black pepper

8 slices whole wheat bread

Sammich fixings (lettuce, tomato, and onion)

This combination of very simple ingredients produces a fresh-tasting salad that is perfect for those summer months when you just couldn't possibly cook. If you can get a just-picked tomato to slice up on top, it is divine. It's kind of like an egg salad sandwich, so use accordingly.

In a large bowl, crumble the tofu with your hands until you reach a crumbly but still somewhat firm consistency. Add the rest of the ingredients (through the pepper) and mix well.

Chill for about 15 minutes. Serve on whole wheat bread spread with a little extra mayo and topped with lettuce, tomato, and onion.

SIDES

I admit I don't get too fussy when it comes to side dishes, so all of these recipes are fairly simple. The most valuable thing about this chapter, though, is the methods, because once you master several cooking methods, you can throw away all your cookbooks (except for the ones I wrote) and start a cooking revolution. So, prepare to roast, bake, braise, and blanch, and we'll cook a little rice while we're at it.

‹‹‹ GINGER ROASTED WINTER
VEGETABLES, PAGE 125

CUMIN-SPICED RICE with TOASTED ALMONDS

3 tablespoons refined coconut oil

¼ cup slivered almonds

1 medium-size onion, cut into ½-inch dice

2 cloves garlic, minced

1 small serrano chile, seeded and finely chopped (or use jalapeño for less heat) (see Fizzle says, page 62)

1 tablespoon minced fresh ginger

2 teaspoons whole cumin seeds

¼ teaspoon whole fennel seeds, crushed (see Fizzle says, page 17)

¼ teaspoon ground cardamom

⅛ teaspoon ground cinnamon

½ teaspoon salt

1½ cups uncooked basmati rice, washed and drained

¼ cup raisins

1 medium-size carrot, grated

I only do up my rice if I'm having friends over; otherwise plain basmati suits me just fine. But when I want to go the extra mile, I make this to go with my Indian-inspired spread. Frying the almonds intensifies the flavor and will have your guests wide eyed and asking what you did to the almonds to make them taste so good. Just shrug and say it's one of life's great mysteries.

Heat a 4-quart pot over medium-high heat. Melt the coconut oil, then cook the almonds, stirring frequently, until golden, about 2 minutes. Transfer with a slotted spoon to paper towels to drain.

Add the onion to the pot and cook over medium-high heat for 5 to 7 minutes, until lightly browned. Add the garlic, chile, ginger, spices, and salt and sauté 1 minute more. Lower the heat and add the rice. Cook for 5 minutes, stirring frequently. Add 2½ cups of water, bring to a boil, then lower the heat. Simmer, uncovered, for about 5 minutes. Add the raisins, cover, and cook over very low heat for 20 more minutes. When most of the liquid has been absorbed, turn off the heat. Add the grated carrots and almonds, mix well, cover, and let sit for 10 more minutes. When the rice is done, fluff with a fork and serve.

COCONUT RICE
WITH TOASTED COCONUT

SERVES 6 TO 8

2 cups jasmine rice, washed

1 (13.5-ounce) can coconut milk

1 cinnamon stick

¼ teaspoon salt

1 teaspoon grated lime zest

2 tablespoons freshly squeezed lime juice

½ cup unsweetened shredded coconut

Lime wedges for garnish (optional)

This is a deceptively easy and tasty dish that looks pretty fancy with the toasted coconut on top. It's a perfect complement to BBQ Pomegranate Tofu (page 165) and it's also great with any Caribbean, Thai, or Indian dish.

Combine the rice, coconut milk, 1 cup of water, the cinnamon stick, and salt in a saucepan and bring to a boil. Lower the heat, cover the pot, and simmer for 20 minutes. Add the lime zest and juice, and stir with a fork. Remove from the heat, cover, and let sit for 10 more minutes.

Meanwhile, prepare the shredded coconut: Heat a dry skillet over low-medium heat. Add the coconut and toast, turning frequently, for about 3 minutes, or until the coconut is browned and toasty.

Remove the cinnamon stick from the rice and serve, sprinkling the toasted coconut over each serving. Garnish with lime wedges, if you so desire.

Fizzle says:

Learning to toast coconut is a skill that will come in handy for so many things, sweet and savory. You can top your ice cream with it, or just sprinkle a handful into a curried soup. It also makes the kitchen smell pretty awesome.

BRUSSELS SPROUT FRIED RICE

2 tablespoons refined coconut oil

12 ounces Brussels sprouts, trimmed and quartered

1 large carrot, peeled and sliced into thin half-moons

¼ cup pine nuts

¼ cup fresh basil leaves

1 cup loosely packed fresh cilantro, chopped

1 cup finely chopped scallion

2 cloves garlic, minced

1 tablespoon minced fresh ginger

4 cups cooked and cooled jasmine rice (see Fizzle says)

¼ teaspoon red pepper flakes

2 tablespoons soy sauce or tamari

1 tablespoon freshly squeezed lime juice

½ teaspoon agave nectar

Sriracha to serve

I put Brussels sprouts in everything. Even fried rice is not safe from that little cruciferous flavor bomb! And until someone invents an even more awesome vegetable, I will continue to overuse them. Not that anyone is complaining.

This version of fried rice is wonderfully aromatic with the addition of fresh herbs and scallions. And a small handful of pine nuts goes a long way to adding another decadent layer of flavor. You can top the dish with some gingery tofu, or toss in some browned tofu, if you'd like it to be an entrée. Or simply serve in addition to a bigger Thai-inspired spread. Or just be like, "It's fried rice for dinner/breakfast/elevenses!" and eat the whole darn thing.

Heat a large, heavy-bottomed pan (preferably cast iron) over medium-high heat. Sauté the Brussels sprouts and carrots in 1 tablespoon of the oil for about 5 minutes, until the Brussels sprouts are lightly charred. Toss in the pine nuts and cook for 2 minutes, tossing often, until toasted. Transfer everything to a large plate and set aside.

Lower the heat to medium and add another teaspoon of oil. Sauté the basil, cilantro, scallions, garlic, and ginger for about a minute, until the herbs wilt slightly and everything smells aromatic and wonderful. Then, add the rice, red pepper flakes, and the remaining 2 teaspoons of oil and cook for about 5 minutes, tossing often.

Add the Brussels mixture back to the pan, and drizzle in the soy sauce, lime juice, and agave. Cook for 3 more minutes or so, until the rice is lightly browned. Taste for salt and adjust, if necessary. Serve with plenty of sriracha!

 *Fizzle says:*

The rice has to be cold for this recipe to work correctly, otherwise it will get mushy and sticky. Many supermarkets carry frozen bags of rice for reasonable prices, and you can make this recipe with a standard 20-ounce bag of rice in mind (Whole Foods has frozen jasmine rice, even). But you can certainly save your pennies and freeze your own ahead of time! Just steam enough to make 4 cups of cooked rice, fluff it, and place in a mesh strainer. Stick the strainer in the fridge to cool completely before freezing—that way, the rice will cook quickly and evenly. Then transfer the rice to a freezer bag and freeze until ready to use. Always keep a bag at the ready for quick weeknight meals, veggie burgers, what have you. For this recipe, you can just toss the rice into the pan frozen.

MASHED POTATOES WITH PUNK ROCK CHICKPEA GRAVY

½ cup unroasted cashews, soaked for at least 2 hours or overnight (see Fizzle says)

½ cup vegan vegetable broth

2 pounds potatoes, cut into 1-inch chunks

1 teaspoon salt (or to taste)

Several dashes of freshly ground black pepper

So easy, so good. Mashed potatoes really need no hype, man—they put on a good show all on their own. I've changed this recipe a bit, opting for cashew cream instead of oils for the creamiest mashed potatoes you ever did eat. I usually use Yukon gold potatoes because they are thin-skinned, but really any potato will work.

Fizzle says:

If you forgot to soak the cashews, have no fear. You can boil them for the same creamy effect. Just submerge in boiling water for 15 minutes, drain, and proceed.

VARIATIONS:

Keep in mind that just about anything can be added to mashed potatoes: chives, curry powder, pesto . . . for example, garlic-wasabi mashed potatoes are mighty yummy . . . the possibilities are endless.

GARLIC MASHED POTATOES: Sauté 4 to 6 cloves of minced garlic in 1½ table-spoons of olive oil and add to the potatoes when you add the cashew cream.

WASABI MASHED POTATOES: Add 1 tablespoon of was-abi to the cashew mixture before blending.

SPINACH MASHED POTATOES: Thaw a package of frozen spinach and pat it dry with a kitchen or paper towel. Add to the potatoes at the end.

Drain the cashews and place in a blender or food processor with the broth. Blend away until completely smooth, occasionally scraping down the sides with a spatula to make sure you get everything. Depending on the strength of your blender, this could take from 1 to 5 minutes.

Place the potatoes in a pot and cover with cold water. Cover and bring to a boil, then add some salt to the water. Re-cover and let boil for 20 minutes or so, until the potatoes are tender.

Drain the potatoes, then add back to the pot. Add the cashew cream, and mash with a potato masher. Add water to thin, if needed, and mash some more until the potatoes are fluffy-ish. Add the salt and black pepper to taste.

CONTINUED >>>

PUNK ROCK CHICKPEA GRAVY

MAKES ABOUT 3 CUPS

¼ cup all-purpose flour

1 tablespoon olive oil

1 medium-size yellow onion, thinly sliced

2 teaspoons whole yellow mustard seeds

3 cloves garlic, minced

2 cups cooked chickpeas, drained (or 1 [16-ounce] can, drained and rinsed)

2 pinches of ground cumin

2 pinches of paprika

Pinch of dried rosemary

Pinch of dried thyme

Pinch of dried oregano

Pinch of ground coriander

3 tablespoons soy sauce

2 tablespoons freshly squeezed lemon juice

¼ cup nutritional yeast

When I do a book signing, this is the recipe people most talk to me about. When I said in the original *Vegan with a Vengeance* that you would make it once a week, I was right! I kind of miss the days when I could just throw everything into a pot and see what happens, because more often than not, awesome stuff like this gravy happens. Truth be told, I hate measuring and all that and am pretty good at eyeballing, but you can't write a whole cookbook that depends on guessing the quantities. Still, you can have one recipe that breaks out, and this is it. I call it "punk rock" because it depends on almost every spice in your spice rack; it would make any "real" chef gasp.

Mix the flour with 2 cups of water until the flour is mostly dissolved.

Heat a large, heavy-bottomed skillet over medium-high heat. Cook the onion and mustard seeds in the olive oil for about 10 minutes, stirring occasionally, until the onion is browned and the seeds are toasted. Add the garlic and sauté for 2 minutes more. Add the chickpeas and use a potato masher to mash them—you don't want to mash them into a paste; just make sure each one is broken up, although if there are a few whole ones left, that is okay. Add the herbs and spices, soy sauce, and lemon juice. Scrape the bottom of the pan to loosen any browned bits of onion.

Lower the heat and pour the flour mixture into the pan. Stir constantly until a thick gravy forms. Stir in the nutritional yeast. If it looks too thick and pasty, add up to ½ cup of water and mix well. It may look as if it wants more water added to it, but just keep mixing and it will loosen up.

Keep warm until ready to serve.

MAPLE–MUSTARD–GLAZED POTATOES AND STRING BEANS

2 pounds small Yukon gold potatoes, halved (about 1-inch pieces)

½ pound string beans, halved, ends cut off and discarded

1 yellow onion, thickly sliced

2 cloves garlic, minced

3 tablespoons tamari or soy sauce

¼ cup pure maple syrup

3 tablespoons Dijon mustard

2 tablespoons olive oil

My best friend, Erica, is the kind of girl who throws a bunch of stuff together, pops it in the oven, forgets about it, goes to her sewing machine, makes a bag, remembers what's in the oven, takes it out, and it's delicious. These potatoes were always a hit at the potlucks, and when people asked for the recipe (and they always asked) she'd be, like, "Potatoes, string beans, garlic, maple syrup, uhhhh, put it in the oven." Having lived with her for several years, I was able to stage several psych ops through which I discerned this recipe.

Preheat the oven to 400°F.

Place the vegetables in a 9 x 13-inch baking dish. In a mixing bowl, stir together all the other ingredients until the mustard is dissolved. Pour over the vegetables and mix well until everything is coated. Cover with foil and place in the oven. Bake for 25 minutes. Remove from the oven and toss everything; use a spoon to drip the sauce over the veggies. Turn down the oven temperature to 350°F, and cook for 25 minutes, uncovered. Remove from the oven, toss again, and cook, uncovered, for 25 more minutes, until tender and golden. These are especially yummy served at room temperature, with some of the remaining sauce poured over them.

SWEET POTATO FRIES

1 tablespoon olive oil

1 teaspoon ground cumin

1 teaspoon ground coriander

¼ teaspoon freshly ground
black pepper

2 large unpeeled sweet potatoes
(about 2 pounds), cleaned and
cut lengthwise into ¼-inch strips

When I started my website the Post Punk Kitchen, readers were able to submit recipes. This was one of the first recipes, submitted by "Beth," and it got positive reviews all around. Reviewers suggested other spices, such as sage or chile powder, so go ahead and be creative with your favorite spices. Even though sweet potatoes and yams are different, it is pretty common to use yams as you do sweet potatoes, so please don't get all technical on me; either one will work in this recipe.

Preheat the oven to 425°F. Lightly grease a large rimmed baking sheet.

Combine the oil, cumin, coriander, and pepper in a large mixing bowl. Add the potatoes and toss well to coat.

Arrange in a single layer on the prepared baking sheet. Bake for 15 minutes. Use tongs to flip the potatoes over, and bake for another 10 to 15 minutes, until browned.

BAKED CAJUN FRENCH FRIES

4 large unpeeled russet potatoes, cleaned and cut lengthwise into ¼-inch strips

2 tablespoons olive oil

2 tablespoons paprika

½ teaspoon ground cumin

¼ teaspoon dried oregano

¼ teaspoon dried thyme

¼ teaspoon cayenne pepper

½ teaspoon coarse sea salt

Nice spicy fries that are baked, not fried. These taste great with any sammich, or by themselves when you're craving a savory snack. Okay, fine, I guess I don't need to tell you what to do with French fries.

Preheat the oven to 450°F. Very lightly grease two large rimmed baking sheets.

In a mixing bowl, toss the potatoes with the olive oil to coat. Mix the spices and salt together and toss with the potatoes to coat. It's okay if the mixture isn't coating every part of each potato; as long as there is some of the spice on each one, you're good.

Arrange the potatoes in a single layer on the prepared baking sheets. Bake for 20 minutes. Use tongs to flip the potatoes, rotate the pans, then bake for another 12 to 15 minutes. The fries should be golden brown. Serve immediately.

ORANGE-GLAZED BEETS

1½ pounds beets (3 to 4 average-size), peeled, quartered, and sliced about ¼-inch thick

1 cup freshly squeezed orange juice

1 teaspoon finely grated orange zest

1 teaspoon pure maple syrup

1 teaspoon salt

The sweetness of the beets is heightened with this simple, tangy orange glaze. I love these alongside mashed potatoes and grilled tempeh. The ingredients are simple but the results are seductively complex.

Place all the ingredients in a large pan, cover, and bring to a low boil. Simmer, stirring occasionally, for about 12 minutes, or until the beets are tender. Uncover and cook until the liquid has reduced to a glaze, about 4 minutes more. These taste great warm, at room temperature, or chilled.

SAUTÉED GREEN BEANS
WITH MUSHROOMS

1 tablespoon olive oil

3 cloves garlic, finely chopped

1½ cups sliced cremini mushrooms

½ teaspoon dried oregano

¼ teaspoon salt

A few dashes of freshly ground black pepper

½ cup vegan vegetable broth

½ cup dry white wine

2½ cups green beans, cut into 1-inch pieces

Garlicky green beans and earthy mushrooms together at last. This is a great Thanksgiving dish or as a side to any Italian meal. You can even add chickpeas or your favorite bean to make it more of an entrée.

Heat a large, heavy-bottomed pan over medium heat. Sauté the garlic in the olive oil for about 2 minutes, stirring frequently. Add the mushrooms, oregano, salt, and pepper, and sauté until the mushrooms begin to release moisture, about 2 minutes. Add the broth and turn the heat up a bit, bringing to a low boil. Simmer for about a minute.

Add the white wine and green beans; cover and simmer for about 2 minutes. Uncover and cook for about 3 more minutes, or until the desired tenderness is reached.

GINGER ROASTED WINTER VEGETABLES

MAKES 6 TO 8 SERVINGS

1 pound parsnips (about 2 average-size), washed, peeled, and cut into ¾-inch chunks

1 pound rutabagas, peeled and cut into ¾-inch chunks

1 pound yellow beets, peeled and cut into ¾-inch chunks

1 pound sweet potatoes (about 3 medium-size), peeled and cut into ¾-inch chunks

2 heaping tablespoons grated fresh ginger

¼ cup pure maple syrup

¼ cup olive oil

¼ teaspoon ground cinnamon

¼ teaspoon ground allspice

1 teaspoon salt

Serve these sweet roasted veggies with garlicky greens and Grilled Tofu (page 159). They are beautiful to behold, and the textures and flavors of the peppery parsnips, the sweetness of the sweetie pots, the earthiness of the beets, and the gingeriness of the ginger will send you into sensory overload. It's just what you want come autumn. The original version of this recipe called for carrots and butternut squash, but I've swapped them out for earthy rutabaga and sweet yellow beets. If you've never tried these vegetables, they may surprise you with their firm texture and sweet/savory flavors.

Preheat the oven to 350°F.

In a large bowl, combine all the ingredients, making sure all veggies are well coated. Doing this with your hands works best.

Place the veggies in a single layer on two large rimmed baking sheets. Pour any extra liquid over the veggies to coat.

Bake for 25 minutes. Remove from the oven, flip the veggies, and rotate the pans. Bake for 20 or so more minutes, until tender and caramelized. Let sit for 10 minutes before serving.

BRAISED CAULIFLOWER WITH THREE-SEED SAUCE

SERVES 4 TO 6

1 large yellow onion, diced small

3 tablespoons olive oil

3 cloves garlic, minced

2 jalapeño peppers, stemmed, seeded, and thinly sliced (see Fizzle says, page 62)

¼ teaspoon salt

2 teaspoons whole cumin seeds

2 teaspoons whole yellow mustard seeds

1 teaspoon whole fennel seeds

½ teaspoon ground turmeric

1 bay leaf

1 large head cauliflower, cut into large florets

1 (16-ounce) can stewed tomatoes

1 teaspoon sugar

Braising is basically sautéing and then steaming in its sauce, and cauliflower takes very well to this process—it stays firm yet tender. This makes a nice side for any Indian-style meal; you can even make it an entrée and serve over basmati rice or with Cumin-Spiced Rice (page 112) if you like.

In a large skillet over medium heat, sauté the onion in the olive oil for 10 minutes. Add the garlic, jalapeños, salt, seeds, spices, and bay leaf; sauté for a minute. Add the cauliflower and sauté for 2 minutes. Add the tomatoes and sugar, stir everything up, cover the pan, and let cook for 5 minutes, stirring occasionally. Uncover and cook for 5 more minutes, until the sauce thickens a bit and the cauliflower is tender but not mushy. Remove the bay leaf. This tastes best if you let it sit for about 10 minutes before serving.

BALSAMIC-GLAZED PORTOBELLO MUSHROOMS

3 medium-size portobello caps, sliced ¼ inch thick

2 tablespoons olive oil

2 tablespoons balsamic vinegar

Pinch of salt

2 cloves garlic, minced

A splash of vinegar enhances these mushrooms to heavenly heights. Garlic adds punch. Tastes great warm, at room temperature, or chilled and used in a salad or sammich. The beauty is in the simplicity. Be careful not to overcook.

Heat a large, heavy-bottomed pan over medium-high heat. Cook the mushrooms in 1 tablespoon of the olive oil in a single layer for about 5 minutes, until they have released moisture. Turn them over and cook for another 2 minutes.

Add the vinegar and salt; sauté for 30 seconds. Add the garlic and the remaining 1 tablespoon of oil, and sauté for 3 more minutes, just until tender.

GARLICKY KALE
WITH TAHINI DRESSING

SERVES 4

6 cloves garlic, thinly sliced

3 tablespoons olive oil

1 pound kale, well rinsed and coarsely chopped

¼ teaspoon salt

Tahini Dressing (page 130)

Lemon wedges to serve

This is the recipe that started my kale journey, and it is still the way I most often serve the leafy green. Lots and lots of garlic, olive oil, and lemon. I always keep tahini dressing in my fridge because it tastes great on everything, but especially for kale purposes.

Sauté the garlic in the olive oil over medium-high heat for about 2 minutes, stirring frequently, until golden brown. Add the kale, the salt, and a few splashes of water. Use tongs to toss the kale around, coating it with the garlic and oil. Cook, stirring frequently, for 4 to 5 minutes.

Serve with a drizzle of Tahini Dressing. I like to use a squeeze bottle for this but if you don't have one, just use a spoon. Garnish with lemon wedges.

Fizzle says:

Any variety of kale is delicious sautéed. Note that lacinato kale will cook faster than green or red curly kale. You can use the stems of the kale if they are on the slender side, about ¼ inch wide. If they are any larger, cut the leaves away from the stem.

CONTINUED >>>

>>> CONTINUED FROM PAGE 128

TAHINI DRESSING

MAKES 2 CUPS

½ cup tahini

2 cloves garlic

¼ cup freshly squeezed lemon juice

1 teaspoon salt

2 tablespoons fresh parsley

This is way more than you need for the Garlicky Kale recipe but I figure if you are making it, might as well have some left over for salad and sammiches or falafel throughout the week. My original Tahini Dressing recipe called for sautéing the garlic and all sorts of things, but this is how I make my tahini now—way easier and just as delicious. Really, just blend a few things and suddenly you have a lush and amazing dressing.

Place all ingredients, except for the parsley, and ¾ cup of water in a blender and blend until smooth. Add extra water, as needed, to thin. (Remember that it will thicken once it's refrigerated, so keeping it on the thin side is not a bad idea.) Pulse in the parsley, taste for salt, and refrigerate until ready to serve.

ROASTED APPLESAUCE

3 pounds red apples
(I like Macintoshes)

2 tablespoons freshly squeezed
lemon juice

2 tablespoons olive oil

⅓ cup pure maple syrup

1 teaspoon ground cinnamon

1 teaspoon grated lemon zest

Pinch of ground allspice

¼ teaspoon salt

This is a standard Passover dish for me to bring as an alternative to regular old applesauce from a jar. It's so much more homey and flavorful. Serve alongside potato pancakes or Horseradish and Coriander–Crusted Tofu (page 166) or anytime you think, "This is good but it could use some applesauce."

Preheat the oven to 400°F.

Peel, core, and slice the apples into 1-inch chunks. Sprinkle with the lemon juice and set aside.

Combine the oil, maple syrup, cinnamon, zest, allspice, and salt in a glass baking dish, and whisk together. Add the apples and toss to coat.

Roast until the apples are very tender, about 25 minutes, turning once after 15 minutes. Transfer to a large bowl and mash. If you prefer a smoother applesauce, you can pulse it a few times in a blender or food processor. You can serve this warm, at room temperature, or chilled.

SESAME ASPARAGUS

2 cloves garlic, minced

1 tablespoon toasted sesame oil

2 tablespoons soy sauce

2 tablespoons rice vinegar

1 teaspoon red pepper flakes

1 pound asparagus,
rough ends discarded

2 tablespoons toasted
sesame seeds

Lightly sautéed asparagus is how I welcome in spring. This recipe is sublime alongside the Asian Tofu (page 159), and served with some jasmine or basmati rice.

Sauté the garlic in the sesame oil over medium heat for about a minute. Add the soy sauce, vinegar, and red pepper flakes. Add the asparagus and sauté for 4 to 5 minutes, until the asparagus is still bright green and firm but slightly tender. Transfer to a serving plate and sprinkle with sesame seeds.

 Fizzle says:

You can toast your own sesame seeds for this recipe. Simply heat the pan you'll be using later to sauté the asparagus (without adding any oil now), and toast the sesame seeds for 3 to 5 minutes, until lightly browned. They won't be uniform in color, but that only adds to the fun. Transfer the seeds to a plate, and then proceed with the rest of the recipe.

ROASTED BRUSSELS SPROUTS
WITH TOASTED GARLIC

1 pound Brussels sprouts, washed and halved

2 tablespoons olive oil

3 cloves garlic, chopped

¼ teaspoon coarse sea salt

Ten years ago you probably thought that we'd have flying cars and time travel by now. No such luck. But you know what has changed more than anything? Everyone's attitude toward Brussels sprouts! Now you need no convincing, the secret is out: Brussels sprouts are the most delicious vegetable ever. Especially when roasted. Especially if you can eat them in your flying car.

Preheat the oven to 400°F.

Lay the Brussels sprouts on a rimmed baking sheet; toss with the olive oil. Roast for 10 minutes. Remove from the oven, add the garlic, and sprinkle with the salt, using tongs to toss to coat. Return to the oven and roast for 5 more minutes. Before you remove the Brussels sprouts from the pan, rub them into the garlic, and, when you serve them, sprinkle them with whatever toasted garlic remains in the pan.

PIZZAS
and
PASTAS

Pizza is the most social food there is. As each pie comes out of the oven, anticipation builds as you wait for it to cool just enough to slice it. The crowds gather, ready to pounce and fight for their slice, if need be. And then everyone sits around eating and saying, "Great pizza!" and coming up with topping ideas for the next one. Or just letting you do all the work. I put pastas here, too, to have a little Italian celebration, and because the sauces can perform double duty as pasta sauces.

‹‹‹ BLT MAC & CHEEZE, PAGE 150

PIZZA DOUGH—A NOVEL

1 cup warm water

1½ tablespoons sugar

1 (¼-ounce) package active
dry yeast

2 tablespoons olive oil, plus about
2 teaspoons for the rising bowl

3 cups all-purpose flour

1 teaspoon salt

Cornmeal

The first step is to "proof" your yeast. Pour the water (be sure it is warm, not hot—"wrist temperature," as they say) into a small bowl and sprinkle in the sugar, then add the yeast. Stir it a little bit so the yeast gets wet, and let it sit in a warm place for 10 minutes or so. When you come back, it should be kind of foamy and maybe even bubbling a bit; if it is, congratulations! Your yeast is alive.

While you're waiting for your yeast to prove itself, you might as well assemble the dry ingredients in a medium-size mixing bowl. Add the oil and the yeast mixture to the flour and salt and stir with a wooden spoon, or mix with your hands if you're the adventurous sort. You won't get very far before the dough balls up and doesn't want to absorb any

more flour; don't worry, that's normal. Sprinkle a little flour on your nice, clean countertop and dump out the whole mixture onto it. It's time to knead.

Kneading dough is a bit more art than science, and there's no real "right" way to do it, as long as you get it thoroughly mixed and stretched. Don't work too hard at it; you're going to be kneading it for 10 minutes or so and you don't want to wear yourself out at the start. A good tip is to use your body weight to lean into it, so that you don't have to work your wrists very hard.

Your dough should be a little sticky; before you start, pat your hands with flour to keep them from sticking. If the dough is really, really sticky, work some more flour into it as you knead. Soon enough the dough should become less sticky and easier to work, in a kind of magical way; now's the time to really start working it, stretching it out and squishing it with your hands. Don't be afraid to treat it rough; that's what the gluten wants. The more you work it, the stretchier and more elastic it will be, which is what you're going for.

After about 10 minutes, the dough should be nice and stretchy, still moist and tacky but not sticky or gooey. If

it seems really tough and dry you've probably added too much flour. Don't worry; it happens. You can still use it; maybe knead it a little longer and remember to try not to add as much flour next time. Pizza dough's not hard, but it takes a little practice to get it perfect.

Form the dough into a tight little ball. You'll need a clean bowl that's at least three times the size of your dough ball for the dough to rise in. I like to use a glass bowl so I can get a real good look at what's going on in there. Put a little oil (about 2 teaspoons, but it doesn't have to be that precise) in the bowl, and put your dough ball in it and swirl it around a little, then flip it over. The idea here is to get both the bowl and your ball of dough covered with a thin film of oil. Cover the bowl with a clean, damp towel or plastic wrap and set it in a warm place. Go away for about an hour.

When you come back, your dough ball should've doubled in size, more or less. Here's the fun part: uncover your dough and give it a firm, solid punch so it deflates. Sprinkle some more flour onto your clean countertop and dump the dough out onto it and start kneading. It should be stretchier and more pliable than it was before.

Knead it for only about a minute, or until it's less like a sponge and more like dough again. Put it back in the bowl and cover it so it can rest.

How long? It's up to you. You can freeze the dough now, if you want, and then defrost it and continue later. If you're impatient, you can wait as little as 10 minutes, but your dough won't be very stretchy. An hour or two would be good. Either way, when you've waited long enough (and when your oven is hot enough; preheat to 500°F or as hot as you dare), sprinkle your countertop with flour (again), take your dough ball out of the bowl, and

cut it in two. Put one portion of dough back into the bowl.

Now it's time to stretch. Like kneading, stretching is an art and you'll get better with practice, so don't be discouraged if your first couple of pizzas are uneven or small. Don't expect to be throwing it up in the air and catching it like they do in the pizzeria; those guys are seasoned pros. Again, there's no right way; whatever works is good, but here's what I do: with my hands, I flatten out the dough a little, and then I roll it out with a rolling pin until it's about a foot in diameter. Then I pick it up on one side and let gravity

help me stretch it out; I work my way around it, trying to stretch it into an even circle, until I start to worry that it will tear. Then I sprinkle my pizza pan with a little cornmeal and set down the crust on it, pat it out a little bit more, and then apply the toppings. If the dough is just right and your stretching technique works, you should be able to get two 14-inch thin-crust pizzas from this recipe; but like I said, it takes practice, so if your pizzas are parallelogram-shaped or lumpy, just say they're "rustic" and don't sweat it.

Now we're ready to make some pizzas!

CLASSIC PESTO

MAKES 1½ CUPS

½ cup walnuts

3 cups packed basil leaves

3 cloves garlic, smashed and coarsely chopped

1½ teaspoons salt

½ cup extra-virgin olive oil, or more to taste

¼ cup nutritional yeast

1 tablespoon freshly squeezed lemon juice

"When in doubt—pesto" is my mantra. I serve it whenever I'm feeling lazy and want to cook something that still has depth and flavor that everyone will love.

Preheat a large pan over medium heat. Toss in the walnuts and toast until fragrant and lightly toasted, about 5 minutes.

Combine the walnuts, basil, garlic, and salt in a food processor or blender and process while you add the olive oil in a slow, steady stream. Add the nutritional yeast and lemon juice, and pulse to combine. The sauce should be the consistency of a slightly grainy paste, not a puree.

PIZZA SAUCE

2 teaspoons olive oil

2 cloves garlic, minced

1 teaspoon dried oregano

½ teaspoon dried thyme

1 teaspoon salt

A few dashes of freshly ground black pepper

1 (22-ounce) can tomatoes in juice (plum tomatoes if you can find them)

2 tablespoons tomato paste

P izza sauce is a simple thing: a little tomato sauce, a little garlic, a few herbs. It doesn't take much to create Brooklyn's most beloved sauce. The mistake some home cooks make is overseasoning it with all kinds of Italian spice mixes and whatnot—all it really needs is a subtle hint of the herbs.

In a saucepan over medium-low heat, sauté the garlic in the olive oil for about 2 minutes, being careful not to burn the garlic. Add the herbs, salt, and pepper. Stir in the tomatoes, crushing them in your hand as you add them. Add about half of the juice from the canned tomatoes and the tomato paste. Increase the heat a bit and cook for about 10 minutes, stirring and crushing the tomatoes as you go. If the sauce looks too chunky, you can use an immersion blender to blend it up a bit, or puree half of it in a blender (just let the sauce cool a bit before putting in into the blender so the steam won't make the lid pop off and splatter hot sauce everywhere). Let cool to room temperature before using on pizzas. You can store whatever you don't use in the fridge for 3 or 4 days, or you can freeze it for up to 3 months.

BASIL-TOFU RICOTTA

MAKES ABOUT 2 CUPS

1 pound firm tofu, pressed
(see page 158)

2 teaspoon freshly squeezed
lemon juice

1 clove garlic, minced

¼ teaspoon salt

Dash of freshly ground black pepper

Handful of fresh basil leaves,
finely chopped (10 leaves or so)

2 teaspoons olive oil

¼ cup nutritional yeast

This is such a versatile recipe. Use as a filling for stuffed shells or lasagne, mixed with tomato sauce in pasta, or as a topping for pizza. You can even dollop it atop salads.

In a large bowl, mush the tofu up with your hands, until it's crumbly.

Add the lemon juice, garlic, salt, pepper, and basil. Mush with your hands again; this time you want it to get very mushy, so squeeze through your fingers and mush until it reaches the consistency of ricotta cheese. This may take 2 to 5 minutes.

Add the olive oil and stir with a fork. Add the nutritional yeast and mix all the ingredients well. Use a fork now, because the oil will make it sticky. Cover and refrigerate until ready to use.

SOME PIZZA TIPS FROM A BROOKLYN GIRL WHO KNOWS FROM PIZZA

+ Don't overload your pizza with toppings, because (a) veggies contain water that will cook out as it heats, and this water can seep into your pizza dough and we don't want that; and (b) the sauce and dough is delicious; it's nice to have an olive here and there, but if olives or mushrooms or what-have-you are all over the thing, it takes away from the pizza experience.

+ Once your pizza dough is prepared, keep it wrapped in plastic wrap—it dries out fast! If it does dry out in some spots, just do your best to rip off the dry parts and use the rest of it.

+ You need a pizza stone for awesome crust. Sure, without one you may be able to get a serviceable crust—but for awesome crust, a stone is a must. Its intense concentrated heat will ensure that you don't wind up with a soggy crust.

+ If you're having trouble stretching out the crust, there's no shame in simply using a rolling pin for the whole shebang. Just be sure that everything is lightly floured so the dough doesn't stick.

+ The best pizza cutters can be found in thrift stores. They have the cutest handles, too.

+ Experiment with textures and flavors. As long as you're not putting worn socks on the pizza, it will probably taste good. I'm giving you a few of my favorite pizzas here, but also try these toppings.

Roasted red peppers

Roasted Brussels Sprouts (page 133)

Pineapple and Tempeh Bacon (page 19)

Artichoke hearts

Roasted garlic (page 74)

POTATO AND TEMPEH SAUSAGE PIZZA

MAKES TWO 14-INCH PIZZAS

Pizza dough for 2 pizzas (page 136)

Pizza Sauce (page 138)

Tempeh Crumbles (page 18)

1 medium-size russet potato, scrubbed, cut in half and thinly sliced (slices should be under ¼ inch thick)

1 tablespoon olive oil, plus extra for drizzling and brushing

1 medium-size fennel bulb, trimmed, very thinly sliced

4 cloves garlic, thinly sliced

Try to cut the potatoes as evenly as possible so that when they cook, they are crispy outside and chewy inside. The fennel and tempeh are a match made in heaven, and the chewy potatoes make the marriage work. I love this pizza as is, but if you would like to add vegan cheese, I can't stop you.

Preheat the oven to 500°F. If using a pizza stone, remember to preheat the oven with the stone inside, on the bottom rack.

Line a large baking sheet with parchment. Toss the potato slices with 1 tablespoon of olive oil and place in a single layer on the baking sheet. Bake for 10 minutes. The potato slices should be very close to tender and lightly browned. Remove from the oven and proceed with recipe.

Roll out your dough as described on page 137. Use the back of a big spoon to spread the pizza sauce onto the dough—use about ⅓ cup or so—leaving about 1½ inches bare around the circumference of the dough. You should still be able to see some of the crust underneath—if you add too much sauce, it may make your dough soggy.

Scatter half of the other toppings randomly over the sauce, making sure that the potato slices and fennel lay flat for even cooking. Drizzle a little olive oil on the garlic, potatoes, and fennel so that they don't dry out while cooking. Use a pastry brush to brush the edge of the crust with a thin layer of olive oil.

Place the crust in the bottom of the oven on a pizza stone. Check it after 8 minutes. Once the crust is lightly browned, your pizza is ready. It can take up to 12 minutes. Remove from the oven and transfer to a large cutting board to slice. Proceed to your next pizza; by this point you should feel like you're fresh off the boat from the Old Country.

Pizza dough for 2 pizzas (page 136)

Pizza Sauce (page 138)

Basil-Tofu Ricotta (page 139)

Classic Pesto (page 137)

⅓ cup pitted and halved kalamata olives

⅓ cup thinly sliced cremini mushrooms

Olive oil for drizzling and brushing

Maybe you've noticed that my name sorta rhymes with pizza? I know someone else who realized that—everyone I've ever met EVER—from my kindergarten class on up. Well, it's finally come in handy! I can name a pizza after myself. Of course, this pizza is awesome or it wouldn't be my namesake: salty olives, fragrant pesto, creamy tofu ricotta, and yummy cremini mushrooms. To get truly Brooklyn-style pizza you'll need to have a metal pizza pan and a pizza stone for the bottom rack of your oven. That will make the crust nice and crisp on the bottom but still chewy and doughy inside. But if you don't have a pizza stone, don't sweat it too much. Simply bake on a regular baking pan and call it a day.

Preheat the oven to 500°F. If using a pizza stone, remember to preheat the oven with the stone inside, on the bottom rack.

Roll your dough onto a pizza pan as described on page 137. Use the back of a big spoon to spread the pizza sauce onto the dough—use about ⅓ cup or so—leaving about 1½ inches bare around the circumference. You should still be able to see some of the crust underneath—if you add too much, it may make your dough soggy. Spoon on the ricotta, in mounds of about 2 tablespoonfuls—you'll want five mounds or so on each pie. Do the same with the pesto. You should have circles of pesto and ricotta but still be able to see the red sauce underneath.

Scatter half of the olives and mushrooms on top of the pizza. Drizzle a little olive oil on the mushrooms so that they don't dry out while cooking. Use a pastry brush to brush the bare crust around the circumference with a thin layer of olive oil.

Place the pizza in the bottom of the oven on a pizza stone. Check it after 8 minutes. Once the crust is lightly browned, your pizza is ready. It can take up to 12 minutes. Remove from the oven and transfer to a large cutting board to slice. Proceed to your next pizza; by this point you should be feeling like a real pizza guy.

GREEN GODDESS GARLIC PIZZA

1 bunch spinach, well rinsed, leaves only

Salt

2 bulbs roasted garlic (page 74)

Pizza dough for 2 pizzas (page 136)

Classic Pesto (page 137)

Green Garden Puree (page 146)

1 tablespoon olive oil, plus extra for drizzling and brushing

½ cup pitted green olives

1 cup chopped broccoli florets

4 cloves garlic, thinly sliced

Cornmeal

This is a delicious and beautiful pizza that is various shades of green and has a delicious roasted garlic base plus more garlic on top for good measure. Because all goddesses should have garlic breath. There are a lot of components here, but you will have the makings for dinner for the next two nights—use the remaining Green Garden Puree and pesto in pasta.

Fill a skillet with about an inch of water and bring to a boil. Add the spinach and sprinkle with salt; cook until the spinach is wilted, about a minute. Drain in a colander and run some cold water over it; when cool enough to handle, press out as much water as you can. Set aside.

Remove the roasted garlic cloves from their skins (you should be able to just squeeze them and the garlic will come out). Place in a bowl and mash with a strong fork. Add a tablespoon of the olive oil and mash into a paste.

Preheat the oven to 500°F. If using a pizza stone, remember to preheat the oven with the stone inside, on the bottom rack.

Roll out your dough as described on page 137. Cover with plastic wrap or a kitchen towel until ready to use.

Spread half of the garlic paste on the pizza dough. Spoon dollops of pesto on top, about 2 inches apart. Spoon on dollops of Green Garden Puree in 2-tablespoon mounds. Place half of the wilted spinach, olives, broccoli florets, and sliced garlic randomly upon the pizza. Drizzle the vegetable toppings with a little olive oil to prevent their drying out. Brush the edge of the crust with olive oil.

Place the pizza in the bottom of the oven on a pizza stone. Check it after 8 minutes. Once the crust is lightly browned, your pizza is ready. It can take up to 12 minutes. Remove from the oven and transfer to a large cutting board to slice. Proceed to your next pizza; by this point you should feel like you're serving pizza in a vegan villa in Italy.

1 pound asparagus, ends discarded, chopped into 3-inch lengths

1 pound green beans, halved, ends removed and discarded

1 cup frozen peas

1 cup slivered almonds

2 cloves garlic

1 cup loosely packed flat-leaf parsley

4 scallions, green parts only, coarsely chopped

2 tablespoons extra-virgin olive oil

Juice of ½ lemon

⅛ teaspoon ground or freshly grated nutmeg

1 pound extra-firm tofu

1 cup chopped basil leaves

This is a fresh-tasting, thick, ricotta-like puree that is delicious as a lasagne or ravioli filling, or as a pasta or pizza topping. It also makes a great straight-up dip with crackers, cut up veggies, or anything else you feel like dipping.

Have ready a large bowl of ice water to "shock" the vegetables.

Bring a large pot of salted water to boil. Add the asparagus and green beans; boil for 2 minutes. Add the frozen peas and boil for 2 more minutes. Drain the vegetables and submerge in the ice water to stop the cooking.

Pulse the almonds into a fine powder. Add the boiled vegetables, garlic, parsley, scallions, olive oil, lemon juice, and nutmeg; puree until smooth.

In a large bowl, mash the tofu with your hands until it has a ricotta-like consistency. Add the puree and mix well. Fold in the basil. Cover and refrigerate until ready to use.

Fizzle says:

Why would anyone want to shock vegetables? I thought vegans were supposed to be nice. All that means is that you toss them into an ice bath after cooking them. This prevents any further cooking and keeps the flavor packed in.

ORECCHIETTE WITH CHERRY TOMATOES AND KALAMATA TAPENADE

SERVES 2 TO 4

FOR THE TAPENADE:

1½ cups kalamata olives, pitted

3 tablespoons capers, drained

2 cloves garlic, chopped

Handful of fresh parsley
(about ½ cup lightly packed)

½ teaspoon dried oregano

½ teaspoon dried tarragon

A few dashes of freshly ground
black pepper

1 tablespoon red wine vinegar

2 tablespoons olive oil

EVERYTHING ELSE:

½ pound orecchiette

1 tablespoon olive oil

1 medium-size red onion, sliced
into thin half-moons (about 1 cup)

1 pound cherry tomatoes, halved

Salty olives and tart, sweet cherry tomatoes taste luscious in this easy-to-prepare dish. I like to use orecchiette here because they cup the thick sauce nicely—but, of course, you can use whatever pasta you want to. This recipe is for a half-pound of pasta, which is supposedly four servings. If you are like most people I know, four servings = two servings, so plan accordingly. The tapenade recipe makes enough for a pound of pasta, though, so you can double the pasta and still have plenty of tapenade-y goodness to go around. If you have some left over, I suggest spreading it on toasted French bread for crostini or adding it to your sandwiches throughout the week.

Prepare the tapenade: Combine all the tapenade ingredients in a blender or food processor. Puree to a spreadable consistency, but not completely smooth.

Prepare the pasta according to the package directions. While the pasta is boiling, sauté the onion and cherry tomatoes in the olive oil over medium heat for about 7 minutes.

Reserve ½ cup of cooking water from the pasta and drain the rest. Add the pasta to the tomatoes and sauté for a few seconds (I use a pasta spoon to sauté because it mixes everything well and doesn't crush anything). Add 1 cup of the tapenade and the reserved pasta water; stir to coat. When the tapenade is heated through, it is ready to serve.

2 pounds russet potatoes, washed and scrubbed

2 tablespoons olive oil

½ teaspoon salt

1½ to 1¾ cups all-purpose flour

Gnocchi are a nice place to start in your pasta-making journey because they are easy, delicious, and pretty difficult to mess up. If you are unfamiliar with gnocchi, they are a small, cute potato dumpling. There are a lot of accoutrements you can spend money on to give your gnocchi the perfect ridges that you find in the store-bought or restaurant variety, but I find that a long fork works just fine. This is my basic recipe to get you started, but I've listed some of my favorite variations below. Make sure to try those as well! Serve with Classic Pesto (page 137), Sun-dried Tomato Pesto (page 191), or a simple tomato sauce.

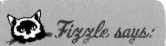

Fizzle says:

The best way to freeze gnocchi and ensure that they don't stick together is to line up the uncooked gnocchi on a parchment-lined cutting board or baking sheet (or anything big and flat) sprinkled lightly with flour. Place the pan in the freezer for about an hour. Then you can transfer the gnocchi to resealable plastic bags or lidded plastic containers and place back in the freezer for up to 3 months. When ready to cook, follow the directions in the recipe.

Preheat the oven to 400°F.

Poke four or five holes all over the potatoes. Bake them (you don't need a tray or foil; right on the oven rack is fine) for 45 minutes to an hour, depending on the size. Do a test after 45 minutes; they should be very, very tender. Clumps are no good for gnocchi, so make sure the potatoes are fully cooked. Use tongs to remove them from the oven; place on a cooling rack and let them cool a bit, just until they are easy to handle. This could take half an hour.

Slice the potatoes in half, scoop the flesh away from the skins (discard the skins), and transfer to a large mixing bowl. Add the olive oil and salt and mash very well. You don't want to puree them—that will make the gnocchi sticky—just mash until relatively smooth. A small avocado masher works well for this. Add the flour in handfuls and incorporate it into the potatoes. Once you've added half of the flour, you can turn the dough onto a floured countertop to work it there. Keep adding flour and lightly kneading the dough until a smooth, unsticky but not dry dough is formed.

Cover in plastic wrap and let rest for 20 minutes or so, in a cool place.

Divide the dough into thirds and roll each portion into a rope that is about ½ inch thick. Use a pizza wheel or a knife to cut the ropes into ¾-inch-long pieces. Now comes the fun part (well, I think it's fun)—flour your hands and use your thumb to roll each piece of gnocchi gently down the tines of a fork. Each piece should be able to do about half a roll before reaching the end of the fork, so the final result should be that one side of the gnocchi has an indent from your thumb and one side has ridges from the fork.

At this point you can sprinkle with flour and freeze any gnocchi you aren't using. To cook them immediately, bring a large pot of water to a boil. Salt the water liberally and cook the gnocchi in three batches. Within 2 minutes they should rise to the surface; let them cook for just under a minute longer and remove them with a slotted spoon. Transfer them to a large plate so that they aren't putting weight on one another and sauce them as soon as you can. I like them with either a simple tomato sauce or sautéed briefly with pesto and veggies.

VARIATIONS:

HERBED GNOCCHI: After mashing the potatoes, add 2 tablespoons of chopped fresh herbs, such as oregano, thyme, and rosemary.

SUN-DRIED TOMATO GNOCCHI: Use only 1½ pounds of potatoes. Soak 1 cup of chopped sun-dried tomatoes in hot water. Cover and let sit until soft, 10 to 15 minutes. Reserve ¼ cup of the soaking water and drain away the rest. Puree the tomatoes in a blender or food processor until smooth, adding the soaking water by the tablespoon, if needed, to achieve a smooth puree. Add the tomatoes to the mashed potatoes. You may need to add ¼ cup or so more flour to the mixture.

SPINACH GNOCCHI: Chop finely one bunch of well-rinsed spinach. Cook in a skillet over medium heat in about ¼ cup of water until it is completely wilted. Place in a strainer and press all the water out. Add to the potatoes after they have been mashed.

BLT MAC & CHEEZE

FOR THE CHEEZE:

1 cup cashews, soaked in water for at least 2 hours or overnight (see Fizzle says, page 117)

1 cup vegan vegetable broth

3 tablespoons nutritional yeast flakes

3 tablespoons freshly squeezed lemon juice

2 teaspoons Dijon mustard

2 teaspoons onion powder

Salt and freshly ground black pepper

FOR THE BLT MAC:

8 ounces small shell pasta or macaroni (gluten-free, whole wheat, or any type)

4 cups baby arugula

2 cups halved cherry tomatoes (or chopped regular tomatoes)

1 recipe Eggplant Bacon (page 152)

BLT Mac & Cheeze! Do I have your attention? If it's summer and you have a garden, or a CSA, or just want to use some in-season produce from the grocery, maybe you can relate to the challenge of Too Many Tomatoes (though, really, can you have too many?). After moving to Omaha, I began growing tomatoes and looked for any reason to put them in everything. And so BLT Mac was born. I made the "B" out of eggplant (remember: vegans will make bacon out of anything). For the "L," arugula is always prolific in the garden, plus I love its muskiness, which goes perfectly with the bright and smoky flavors of the other ingredients.

TO MAKE THE CHEEZE:

Drain the cashews and place with all the sauce ingredients in a blender or food processor and blend away until completely smooth. Scrape down the sides with a spatula to make sure you get everything. Depending on the strength of your blender, this could take from 1 to 5 minutes. Taste for salt and pepper, keeping in mind that you want it just a little saltier than you think because it's going to be poured over all of the other ingredients.

TO MAKE THE BLT MAC:

Prepare the pasta according to the package directions. When the pasta is tender, drain it in a colander. Immediately place it back in the pot you boiled it in and stir in the sauce. Place the pot on low heat and stir for 3 minutes or so, until the sauce is thickened a bit and everything is deliciously creamy. Taste for salt again.

Now toss in the arugula, tomatoes, and eggplant bacon, leaving a little extra aside to garnish, if you like.

EGGPLANT BACON

1 pound eggplant

Cooking spray

¼ cup soy sauce or tamari

1 teaspoon liquid smoke

This recipe is so easy you'll be making eggplant bacon in your sleep! The perfect slice has varying textures from crisp and browned in some spots, to tender and chewy in others. To that end, hand slice these babies instead of using a mandoline and aim for ⅛-inch slices, but don't worry about perfection. The varying degrees of thickness will work to your advantage here. Just don't cut it too thick, the eggplant needs to crisp up, and slices that are much thicker will just get soggy.

Preheat the oven to 425°F. Line two large baking sheets with parchment paper.

Prep the eggplant while the oven is preheating. Eggplants vary in size, so if using baby eggplant that is 2 inches wide at its widest, just slice into ⅛-inch-thick circles. If using large eggplants, first cut in half lengthwise, then slice the halves into ⅛-inch-thick half-moons. Now, what we're going to do is bake it at a high temperature with just a bit of cooking spray, then let it cool, then give it smoky salty flavor and reheat.

Spray the lined baking sheets lightly with cooking spray. Arrange the eggplant pieces in a single layer and spray lightly once more. Place in the oven and bake for about 8 minutes, keeping a close eye. Rotate the pans about halfway through baking.

Remove from the oven and flip the slices. They should be browning already, and if any are slightly burnt, don't worry; just transfer them to a plate to cool. Return the remaining strips to the oven for about 3 minutes.

Remove from the oven. The eggplant should be dark brown to burnt in some places, and yellowish white and tender in some places. Transfer to a plate to prevent further baking.

Lower the oven temperature to 350°F. Mix the soy sauce and liquid smoke together in a large bowl. Dip the eggplant slices in mixture a few at a time and return to the baking sheet. Bake for about 3 more minutes, until heated through. Serve!

Keeps well for a few more hours, but definitely use these the day of.

FETTUCCINE ALFREDA

8 ounces fettuccine

2 teaspoons olive oil

1 medium-size onion, chopped into big chunks

4 cloves garlic, chopped

½ cup water or vegan vegetable broth

2 teaspoons yellow mustard

½ cup pine nuts, toasted (see Fizzle says)

2 teaspoons soy sauce or Bragg Liquid Aminos

2 teaspoons chile powder

1 cup nutritional yeast

½ teaspoon salt

A few dashes of freshly ground black pepper

Fizzle says:

To toast pine nuts, heat a heavy-bottomed skillet over medium-high heat. Toss in the pine nuts and stir frequently for about 5 minutes, until they are lightly browned.

This recipe is from my old friends the Baltimorons, but by the time this recipe was invented, they had moved to Minneapolis. Anyway, one of them found a bag of pine nuts and they taught me to make this sauce, or something like it. I can't exactly duplicate the recipe because I think a lot of the flavor came from the fact that the pine nuts were "found." It's yummy to add some sautéed veggies on top of the pasta, and some grilled Marinated Tofu (page 159) wouldn't hurt, either. Serve it with some home brew that may not have come out quite right. For the record, most people (myself included) don't think that this tastes like a dairy alfredo. But it is an amazing, unique pine nut sauce that found its way into many people's weekly rotation, despite the misnomer.

Prepare the pasta according to the package directions.

Heat a large, heavy-bottomed pan over medium heat. Sauté the onion in the olive oil for 3 minutes, until just slightly softened. Add the garlic and sauté for 2 more minutes. Transfer to a blender, add all the other ingredients, and blend away. It should be somewhat smooth but still a bit grainy.

This amount should be enough for four servings of pasta. You can reheat it in a saucepan over low heat, if you need to. If you want to make it thicker, add more nutritional yeast by the tablespoon. To thin it out, add pasta water by the tablespoon.

Drain the pasta and transfer it to a plate, spoon the sauce over the top, add veggies and tofu, if using, and serve.

CREAMY RED CHARD LINGUINE

8 ounces linguine
(I use whole wheat)

½ cup cashews, soaked in water
for at least 2 hours or overnight
(see Fizzle says, page 117)

1¾ cups vegan vegetable broth

¼ cup pine nuts

2 tablespoons olive oil

1 red onion, thinly sliced

4 cloves garlic, thinly sliced

4 cloves garlic, minced

1 teaspoon dried thyme

½ teaspoon red pepper flakes

Freshly ground black pepper

½ teaspoon salt

1 pound red Swiss chard, leaves
torn into bite-size pieces, stems
thinly sliced

½ cup dry red wine (Merlot works
great)

2 tablespoons freshly squeezed
lemon juice

File under simple but impressive! When cooking with chard, I like to use the whole animal. The beautiful red stems and some red wine make this pasta a fun pink hue. This pasta is all about color and texture—cashews makes it rich and creamy, while Swiss chard is delightfully chewy, and toasted pine nuts provide crunchy explosions of flavor. I've also used a ton of garlic two ways, sliced and minced, so be prepared for serious garlic love!

Cook the linguine according to the package directions, then drain. (While the pasta is cooking, you can proceed with the rest of the recipe.)

Drain the soaked cashews and then puree them, with 1¼ cups of the broth, in a blender or food processor until completely smooth. Scrape down the sides occasionally with a spatula to make sure you get everything. It might take from 1 to 5 minutes to get it really smooth.

Heat a large pan over medium heat. Toast the pine nuts until browned, about 3 minutes. Remove from the pan; place in a small bowl (or whatever), and set aside.

In the same pan, sauté the onion in the oil and a pinch of salt for about 5 minutes. Add the sliced garlic and sauté

for 2 more minutes. Add the minced garlic, thyme, red pepper flakes, black pepper, and salt and sauté for a minute more. Add the Swiss chard stems (reserve the leaves) and sauté for another 2 minutes.

Pour in the wine and remaining ½ cup of broth and turn up the heat to bring to a boil. Let reduce for about 5 minutes. Lower the heat and add the Swiss chard leaves. Cook until they are completely wilted.

Add the cashew cream and lemon juice and stir until heated through. Taste for salt and pepper.

By this time, the pasta should be cooked and drained. Add it to the pan, turn off the heat, and toss to coat. Serve as soon as you can and top with the pine nuts.

ENTRÉES

I can never answer the question "What is your favorite kind of food?" because, well, "favorite" questions are sort of arbitrary and there are just too many answers to choose from. Yet people always seem to ask. My standard answer is "Brooklyn food," because it seems like there isn't one culinary palate that dominates my beloved borough. So, here you will find a diverse selection of dishes inspired by every corner of the world, and I never had to leave Brooklyn for inspiration.

‹‹‹ SEITAN-PORTOBELLO STROGANOFF, PAGE 172

MARINATED TOFU

I eat some version of the following recipes for dinner a few times a week because they are so easy yet produce amazing results. It's hard to remember that simple things can be extraordinary but these recipes prove just that.

I've listed a few marinade recipes and you can use either the baking or grilling instructions. Baking produces a firmer tofu, and the flavors are a little bit more concentrated. Grilling produces a caramelly char. Both methods have their place, depending on what you're in the mood for. Generally, I bake in the winter and grill in the summer, when I don't want to turn the oven on.

TAMING YOUR TOFU

Tofu is a delicious protein that can be quite versatile once you get the hang of using it. If you've been unsuccessful using it in the past, try these tips and I guarantee you will be a tofu pro in no time (well, in about the hour it takes to press it).

The most important thing to know when dealing with tofu is that for a nice, firm texture, you will need to press all the water out. This will allow any marinade you soak it in to penetrate as much as possible, and will help it to crisp up when frying.

Start with a drained block of extra-firm tofu and place it between a clean kitchen towel or three or four paper towels on each side. Place a heavy, level object (such as a hardcover book) over the tofu. For good measure you can place another heavy object on top of the book. I often use a few cans of beans or sometimes a cast-iron pan. Let it sit like that for half an hour, then flip it over for another half-hour.

If you don't have a full hour to press the tofu, you can "quick press" it. Cut it into four equal slices widthwise and press each slice very gently between your hands to get the water out. Then wrap each slice in paper towels and place under a heavy object as described above for as long as you can (at least 10 minutes).

Freezing tofu creates a different, chewier texture. Freeze it in its packaging and let it thaw completely before pressing it. It's very important that the tofu thaws completely or else it will have a spongy unappealing texture. Frozen tofu tastes great crumbled into chilis and stews.

Don't limit your tofu cuts to dices and thin rectangles. Following are some of my favorite ways to slice tofu. I find that different shapes and sizes can really up the visual aspects of any dish.

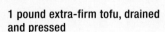

ASIAN TOFU

1 pound extra-firm tofu, drained and pressed

½ cup mirin

3 tablespoons tamari

2 tablespoons rice wine vinegar

1 tablespoon sesame oil

2 teaspoons Asian chile sauce

1 (1-inch) chunk ginger, peeled and coarsely chopped

2 cloves garlic, smashed

This tofu goes great with Wasabi Mashed Potatoes (page 117) and asparagus. It's also great in sandwiches. To make it into a sort of Banh Mi, just add pickles, mayo, sriracha, and mint.

FOR THE MARINADE:

Prepare your marinade of choice: Combine all the marinade ingredients in a wide, shallow bowl.

FOR GRILLED TOFU:

Cut the tofu widthwise into four equal pieces. Marinate for an hour, flipping over after 30 minutes.

Grease a stovetop grill pan (preferably cast iron) with vegetable oil. Heat over a high flame for about 3 minutes. To get those perfect grill marks, make sure that your grill is smoking hot and lightly greased before throwing the tofu on. A cold pan will lead to lackluster grill marks or make the tofu stick. So, don't be afraid of a little smoke and heat! That's kitchen life. Use tongs to distribute the tofu slabs evenly on the grill. Gently use the tongs to press the tofu into the grill ridges, to get nice dark lines. Cook for

3 minutes on one side without lifting, then turn the slabs 90 degrees to create a crosshatched pattern on the bottom of the tofu. Cook for 2 minutes, then flip over and cook for another 2 minutes. Transfer to a cutting board and cut each piece diagonally across into two triangles with a sharp knife. (See "Taming Your Tofu," page 158.)

FOR BAKED TOFU:

Preheat the oven to 400°F.

Cut the tofu widthwise into eight equal pieces. Marinate for an hour, flipping after 30 minutes.

Place the tofu on a baking sheet and bake for 20 minutes. Flip over and bake for another 10 minutes. Place in the broiler for about 3 more minutes, for extra chewiness.

1 pound extra-firm tofu, drained and pressed

½ cup white cooking wine

2 tablespoons olive oil

2 tablespoons balsamic vinegar

2 tablespoons Bragg Liquid Aminos or tamari

2 tablespoons freshly squeezed lemon juice

2 cloves garlic, smashed

A big pinch of dried basil

A big pinch of marjoram

A big pinch of thyme

This is the tofu you want on top of pasta, smothered in pesto or marinara. And if you're not doing the pasta thing, it's also great with quinoa, farro, rice . . . any grain, really!

Follow directions for Asian Tofu on page 159.

Fizzle says:

Don't throw the tofu out with the bathwater; reserve your marinade and get creative. Remove the garlic and/or ginger and mix in a little water and arrowroot or cornstarch, then heat it up and you've got yourself a gravy. Or use it to stir-fry broccoli or asparagus for a nice, fast side dish: heat some vegetable oil over high heat, then add your chopped vegetables, pouring on splashes of the marinade as you cook.

TOFU CHIMICHURRI

FOR THE CHIMICHURRI:

4 cloves garlic

1 cup loosely packed fresh cilantro

1 cup loosely packed fresh parsley

1 teaspoon dried oregano

¼ cup red wine vinegar

2 tablespoons olive oil

1 tablespoon soy sauce or tamari

½ teaspoon red pepper flakes

½ teaspoon salt

¾ cup vegan vegetable broth

EVERYTHING ELSE:

14 ounces tofu, pressed and sliced widthwise into 8 slices

Cooking spray

Chimichurri is, first and foremost, fun to say. Beyond that, it's a fresh and acidic green sauce made from herbs and spices and, although in Argentina it's reserved for steak, us vegans use it on tofu! When marinated, it sucks up the sauce beautifully, and then you use the leftover marinade to pour right over the cooked tofu. So fresh and flavorful! You can serve this over mashed potatoes with lots of green veggies, or over the Ginger Roasted Winter Vegetables (page 125).

To make the chimichurri, simply blend all of the sauce ingredients until relatively smooth. Transfer to a mixing bowl.

Place the tofu slices in the chimichurri and marinate for an hour or so, flipping once.

Preheat a large, heavy-bottomed pan over medium-high heat. Spray the pan with a thin layer of cooking spray.

Place the tofu in a single layer and cook for 4 minutes or so, until lightly browned. Spray with more spray, and flip the tofu, cooking for 3 more minutes. Now turn off the heat and add the reserved marinade and flip the tofu around to coat, just to warm up the sauce.

Serve covered in chimichurri from the pan.

2 tablespoons organic cornstarch

1 cup cold vegan vegetable broth

2 cups thinly sliced cremini mushrooms

4 tablespoons olive oil

1 large yellow onion, quartered and thinly sliced

4 cloves garlic, coarsely chopped

½ teaspoon dried thyme, chopped

A few dashes of freshly ground black pepper

1½ cups dry white wine

1 tablespoon tamari or soy sauce

3 tablespoons chickpea miso

1 pound Yukon gold potatoes, cut into 1-inch chunks

1 pound tofu, pressed, cut into eighths widthwise, and then cut into two long isosceles triangles (see page 158)

Fizzle says:

Little tiny potatoes work really well here! If they're about egg-size, you only need to cut them in half for this stew. Then it's like no prep work at all.

Even though this recipe calls for miso, it has a very midwestern "meat and potatoes" taste and texture. The potatoes are perfectly creamy yet still firm and the tofu is deliciously plump and packed with flavor. The gravy thickens as it cooks until it's lush and creamy. I love that it comes together so easily and cooks in one pan without any fuss. I use chickpea miso, but really you can use any that you have on hand. Serve with some broccoli and brown rice.

Mix the cornstarch with the broth to dissolve, and set aside.

In a large skillet, sauté the mushrooms in 2 tablespoons of the olive oil over medium-high heat for 5 to 7 minutes, until browned and most of the water has evaporated. Remove from the pan and set aside.

Sauté the onion in the remaining 2 tablespoons of olive oil for 5 to 7 minutes, until slightly browned; add the garlic, thyme, and black pepper and sauté for 2 more minutes. Stir in the white wine, cornstarch mixture, tamari, and miso. Bring to a boil, then lower the heat to a simmer; the miso should be completely dissolved. Add the mushrooms, potatoes, and tofu. The pan will be crowded, but make sure that all potatoes are mostly submerged in the gravy; it's okay if they stick out a little. Cover and simmer over low heat for 25 to 30 minutes, until the potatoes are very tender.

Turn off the heat and wait about 10 minutes before serving, for the flavors to meld.

BBQ POMEGRANATE TOFU

FOR THE TOFU:

2 (14-ounce) blocks extra-firm tofu, drained and pressed, sliced widthwise into eighths

2 tablespoons peanut oil

1 tablespoon tamari

FOR THE BBQ SAUCE:

1 tablespoon peanut oil

1 cup minced shallots

2 cloves garlic, minced

½ teaspoon Chinese five-spice powder

2 cups vegan vegetable broth

A few dashes of freshly ground black pepper

1 (6-ounce) can tomato paste

2 tablespoons creamy all-natural peanut butter

2 tablespoons pomegranate molasses

2 tablespoons tamari or soy sauce

¼ cup pure maple syrup

1 teaspoon sriracha (or to taste)

1 teaspoon liquid smoke

FOR GARNISH:

½ cup pomegranate seeds

I love the floral taste of pomegranate and a little molasses goes a long way. I realize pomegranate molasses is an esoteric ingredient, but it's one of those things I was dying to try and it was well worth hunting out. I was even able to find it at the shabby grocery store near my apartment, but I think any well-stocked gourmet store will have it; if not, try Amazon. (And order some gourmet salts while you're at it, they're fun.) I like to steam some veggies to go along with it and smother them in the extra sauce; served with the Coconut Rice (page 113), you've created something sublime.

Prepare the tofu: Preheat the oven to 350°F. On a large rimmed baking sheet, dredge the tofu in the peanut oil and tamari to coat on both sides. Bake for 15 minutes, then flip the slices and bake for 15 minutes more.

Meanwhile, prepare the BBQ sauce: In a saucepan over medium heat, sauté the shallots in the peanut oil for about 5 minutes, add the garlic and five-spice powder, and sauté for 1 minute more. Add the broth and bring to a simmer. Add the rest of the ingredients (except for the pomegranate seeds) and bring to a boil. Lower the heat and simmer for 15 to 20 minutes, stirring frequently.

At this point, your tofu should be done baking. Smother the tofu with the BBQ sauce, return to the oven, and bake for 15 minutes more. Remove from the oven. Serve with Coconut Rice and garnish with the pomegranate seeds.

Fizzle says:

If you don't want to get a whole jar of pomegranate molasses, you can replace it with regular old molasses and there you go—still a yummy BBQ flavor.

HORSERADISH AND CORIANDER—CRUSTED TOFU

FOR THE MARINATED TOFU:

½ cup dry white wine

1 tablespoon tamari or soy sauce

¼ cup freshly squeezed lemon juice

2 cloves garlic, smashed

14 ounces extra-firm tofu, drained
and pressed for at least an hour,
sliced widthwise into eighths

FOR THE CRUST:

⅓ cup vegan panko (Japanese
bread crumbs; if you can't find
these, use unflavored, vegan,
preferably whole wheat bread
crumbs)

⅓ cup very loosely packed chopped
fresh mint

3 tablespoons grated fresh
horseradish

Finely grated zest of 1 lemon

1 tablespoon coriander seeds,
crushed (see Fizzle says, page 17)

⅛ teaspoon salt

A few dashes of freshly ground
black pepper

1 tablespoon oil

Most people are familiar with horseradish of the jarred variety, and that's all fair and well, but it's a whole other thing to experience this spicy root freshly grated. With the fresh mint and the lemon zest, this is just bursting with flavor after flavor. I originally stole this basic recipe from a fish cookbook, so I serve it with a simple tartar sauce (2 parts vegan mayo, 1 part sweet pickle relish) and Wasabi Mashed Potatoes (page 117). For a green veg, grilled asparagus is a good choice if you wanna keep it fancy.

Prepare the marinated tofu: Mix all the ingredients together in a shallow bowl; marinate the tofu for at least 1 hour, turning occasionally.

While the tofu is marinating, preheat the oven to 400°F. Line a baking pan with foil and lightly coat in oil or spray with nonstick cooking spray.

Prepare the crust mixture: In a shallow bowl, mix together the bread crumbs, mint, horseradish, lemon zest, coriander, salt, and black pepper. Sprinkle with the olive oil and combine with a fork.

Press each piece of tofu firmly into the crust mixture on both sides, one piece at a time. Take a small amount of the crust mixture and press it into the top side of the tofu (the underside will be less crusty because less crumbs stick to it; just a little sprinkle of crumbs should suffice on that side, otherwise too many will burn). Place each slice in the prepared pan.

Bake for 15 minutes. Transfer to the broiler and broil for 5 minutes. Serve.

Fizzle says:

Once the horseradish is grated, be prepared to use it immediately; it will develop a bitter taste if left around for too long.

MANGO-GINGER TOFU

FOR THE MARINADE AND SAUCE:

2 teaspoons peanut oil

3 cloves garlic

¼ cup coarsely chopped fresh ginger

1 jalapeño pepper, seeded and chopped (see Fizzle says, page 62)

2 large mangoes, peeled and coarsely chopped (see Fizzle says)

¼ cup pure maple syrup

1 cup dry white wine

2 tablespoons rice vinegar

¼ cup freshly squeezed lime juice

1 cup freshly squeezed orange juice

¼ teaspoon ground allspice

½ teaspoon salt

Freshly ground black pepper

FOR THE TOFU:

2 (14-ounce) blocks extra-firm tofu, drained and pressed, cut into 8 slices each widthwise

1 red bell pepper, seeded and cut into long, thin slices

1 mango, sliced into long, thin slices

The summer that I invented this mango tofu, little could stop me from bringing it to any function that would have me. I started to get self-conscious that people might think it was the only thing I knew how to make, and they'd start calling me "Isa with the mango tofu," but really it's that good. Choose mangoes that are ripe but not overripe; they should give only slightly if you squeeze them.

Prepare the marinade: Heat a 4-quart pot over medium heat; sauté the garlic, ginger, and jalapeño in the peanut oil for 7 minutes. Add the chopped mango and sauté for 5 more minutes.

Add the maple syrup and wine, cover, and simmer for 35 minutes. Uncover and simmer for 5 more minutes.

Fizzle says:

The easiest way to chop a mango is also the messiest way. First, peel with a serrated peeler to prevent slipping. Then place on a cutting board, slice against the flat part of the pit, and repeat on the other sides. Then simply chop the fruit slices as needed.

Turn off the heat. Add the vinegar, lime juice, orange juice, allspice, salt, and black pepper; let cool a bit, then transfer the mixture to a blender and puree until smooth.

Place the tofu in the marinade in a resealable plastic bag or a tightly lidded plastic container. Marinate in the fridge for at least 3 hours and up to overnight. After the tofu is nearly done marinating, preheat the oven to 375°F.

Reserve half of the marinade. Lay the marinated tofu in a single layer in a lightly greased large rimmed baking sheet. Bake for 20 minutes. Flip over the tofu and add more marinade. Coat the red pepper and sliced mango in the reserved marinade and add them to the pan. Bake for another 15 minutes.

Heat the remaining marinade in a saucepan and put in a bowl so guests can pour it over the tofu. Serve over jasmine rice with a steamed vegetable.

PUMPKIN SEED–CRUSTED TOFU WITH BAKED PUMPKIN AND CRANBERRY RELISH

SERVES 3 TO 4

1 (3-pound) sugar pumpkin

2 tablespoons canola oil, plus extra for shallow frying

½ cup organic cornstarch

¼ cup fresh oregano, chopped

¼ teaspoon salt

1 cup all-purpose flour

1 pound extra-firm tofu, drained and pressed, sliced lengthwise into eighths

Cranberry Relish (recipe follows)

I used to buy a couple of pumpkins every year with plans to cook them in some extravagant way. Even if I had the best intentions, they'd end up as decoration until they met their demise. Not anymore! As much as I love winter squash, it just used to intimidate me, until this recipe, which utilizes the whole pumpkin—the pulp and the seeds. It's fun to pull together and it's got that homespun feel because you toast the seeds yourself. It's also really crunchy and flavorful, especially topped off with the cranberry relish. I hope this becomes an autumn tradition for you as it has for me.

Preheat the oven to 300°F.

Carve out the top of the pumpkin with a paring knife and slice the pumpkin in half with a chef's knife. Remove the seeds and clean them in a strainer under running water (the holes should be big enough for the stringy bits to escape). Set the pumpkin aside to prepare as described below. Dry the seeds thoroughly by laying on a paper towel or kitchen towel; pat the tops with another towel to remove any moisture. Measure ¾ cup of seeds and transfer them to a rimmed baking sheet. Sprinkle with 2 teaspoons of the oil and toss to coat. Bake for 20 minutes, flipping occasionally. They should be toasted a golden brown to a deep golden brown. Transfer to a bowl to cool. (If there are more seeds left over, roast them the same way for a snack.)

Meanwhile, prepare the pumpkin: Increase the oven temperature to 350°F. Cut the pumpkin into slices that are about 2 inches wide at the widest point. Lightly oil the slices with canola oil. Place on a rimmed baking sheet and bake for about 45 minutes, until tender and lightly browned.

When the seeds have cooled, transfer them to a food processor and pulse until crumbly; the texture should range from ground to coarse and chunky. In a shallow bowl, mix the seeds with the cornstarch, oregano, and salt. Place the flour in another bowl, and 1 cup of water in another, and line up your three bowls: flour, water, and the seed mixture.

Heat ¼ inch of oil over medium heat in a heavy-bottomed skillet, preferably cast iron. The heat should be between 320° and 350°F; if you don't have a thermometer, test the oil by dropping a pinch of the seed mixture in; if bubbles form rapidly around the seeds, the oil is ready.

Dip the tofu on both sides into the flour, then into the water, then into the seed mixture on both sides until the tofu is well coated with seeds. Repeat until all eight pieces are coated. Using tongs, lower the pieces into the oil (you may have to do it in two batches). Fry for 3 minutes on one side and

about 2 minutes on the second side. Remove from the oil and transfer to flattened paper bags or paper towels to drain the excess oil. Serve with roasted pumpkin and cranberry relish.

 *Fizzle says:*

When frying, the temperature of the oil is really important. Too hot and the food will burn; too cool and it won't cook properly. A frying thermometer is a pretty important accessory to have for this kind of stuff. If you don't have one, there are several methods to test whether the oil is ready. One is to drop in some crumbs and see whether bubbles form around it quickly; if the bubbles are out of control and smoky, it's too hot. If they are slow to form, the oil may need more heat or just a little more time. You can also use a wooden spoon: dunk in the handle and if bubbles quickly surround it, the oil is ready.

CRANBERRY RELISH

MAKES 2½ CUPS

2 cups fresh cranberries, coarsely chopped

½ cup pure maple syrup

¼ cup freshly squeezed orange juice

1 teaspoon finely grated orange zest

Mix together all the ingredients plus ½ cup of water in a small saucepan. Cover and bring to a boil. Once boiling,

uncover and let simmer for 15 minutes. Bring to room temperature and serve.

SEITAN

FOR THE BROTH:

12 cups water or vegan vegetable broth

½ cup soy sauce

FOR THE SEITAN:

2 cups vital wheat gluten flour, plus extra if needed

⅓ cup nutritional yeast

1 cup cold water or vegan vegetable broth

½ cup soy sauce

1 tablespoon tomato paste

1 tablespoon olive oil

2 cloves garlic, pressed or grated on a Microplane grater

1 teaspoon finely grated lemon zest

In traditional seitan, the wheat flour is washed and kneaded three times over two days to develop the wheat gluten. I speed things up in this recipe by using vital wheat gluten flour. The first time I made seitan, I used a recipe from the cookbook *Vegan Vittles*. This recipe was inspired by that one, but has been modified over the years. I've changed my method of seitan making over the past decade to troubleshoot some of the problems people were having while making it, so I hope that this foolproof method produces the perfect seitan of your dreams!

Prepare the broth: In a large pot that holds at least 6 quarts, bring the water and soy sauce to a boil.

In the meantime, prepare the seitan: In a large bowl, mix together the vital wheat gluten flour and nutritional yeast. Make a well in the center and add the remaining seitan ingredients: water, soy sauce, tomato paste, olive oil, garlic, and zest.

Combine with a fork until a dough forms, then knead the dough for about 5 minutes, until spongy and elastic. If it feels soggy, you may need to add a few more tablespoons of vital wheat gluten flour.

The broth should be boiling by now; turn down the heat to a low simmer. Roll the dough into a log shape about 10 inches long and cut it into six

pieces of roughly equal size. Place the pieces in the broth. Partially cover the pot (leave a little space for steam to escape) and make sure that the broth comes back to a gentle simmer after the seitan is added.

Simmer for an hour, turning the pieces every now and again.

Turn off the heat and let the broth and seitan cool for at least 30 minutes. This will produce a firmer seitan. It is best to let everything cool completely before removing the seitan from the broth.

What you do next depends on the recipe you are using. If storing the seitan for later use, slice it into bite-size chunks, put it into a sealable container, and cover with broth. Seal the container and place it in the fridge for up to 5 days.

JERK SEITAN

FOR THE MARINADE:

½ large white onion, coarsely chopped

2 cloves garlic, crushed

2 tablespoons peeled, roughly chopped fresh ginger

3 tablespoons freshly squeezed lime juice

3 tablespoons soy sauce

2 tablespoons olive oil

2 tablespoons pure maple syrup

2 teaspoons dried thyme

1 teaspoon ground allspice

¼ teaspoon ground cinnamon

¼ teaspoon cayenne pepper

1 teaspoon ground or freshly grated nutmeg

FOR THE SEITAN:

2 cups seitan (page 170), cut into thick strips

2 teaspoons olive oil

1 onion, thickly sliced (about 1 cup)

1 green bell pepper, seeded and thickly sliced

My favorite Brooklyn soul food restaurant closed without warning one day and I was left pressing my face against the glass, hoping against hope that it might somehow open again, but it never did. It served the best jerk sauce known to woman. So, I took matters into my own hands and came up with this dish that satisfies my cravings quite nicely. It's spicy and herby and tangy and just plain jerky. This is the sort of recipe you can really play around with to your tastes. I rely on dried spices and pantry staples that are easy to replace; the lime can be subbed with 3 tablespoons of apple cider vinegar; the maple syrup can be subbed with sugar. All the marinade ingredients are going to be blended together, so don't be too finicky about your chopping.

Prepare the marinade by pureeing all the ingredients in a blender or food processor until relatively smooth. There will be some chunkiness but that's okay.

Add the seitan: Place the seitan in a shallow bowl and pour that marinade over it. Mix to coat. Cover and let marinate for an hour.

When the seitan is done marinating, in a large skillet, sauté the onion and bell pepper in the olive oil over medium-high heat for 5 to 7 minutes, until the onion starts to brown. Remove the seitan from the marinade and reserve the liquid. Add to the onion mixture and sauté for 10 minutes, until the seitan has browned to your liking. Add the remaining marinade and cook for about 2 minutes to heat the sauce through.

Serve with Coconut Rice (page 113), sautéed greens, and baked sweet potatoes or roasted autumn vegetables; ladle the extra sauce over each serving.

SEITAN-PORTOBELLO STROGANOFF

2 tablespoons organic cornstarch

2 cups cold vegan vegetable broth

4 cups seitan (page 170), sliced into ¼-inch-thick strips

4 tablespoons olive oil

2 cups thinly sliced shallots

3 cloves garlic, minced

2 cups cremini mushrooms, thinly sliced

2 portobello caps, thinly sliced

2 tablespoons fresh thyme, chopped

½ pound fettuccine

2 teaspoons salt

1 cup dry red wine

1 tablespoon sweet paprika

½ cup nutritional yeast

½ cup unsweetened almond milk (or preferred nondairy milk)

2 teaspoons Dijon mustard

1 cup frozen green peas

Chopped fresh parsley for garnish (optional)

Here's everything you want in a stroganoff: noodles and peas, meatiness, and of course creamy mushroom goodness. The red wine, shallots, and fresh thyme give the sauce lots of depth, but the recipe isn't complicated, so it's perfect for date night or just a cozy family meal. Definitely use homemade seitan here, and make it the day before so that dinner will come together quickly.

Dissolve the cornstarch in the 2 cups of broth; set aside.

Heat a large, cast-iron pan over medium-high heat. Sauté the seitan in 2 tablespoons of olive oil until lightly browned, about 5 minutes. Transfer the seitan to a plate and set aside. Return the pan to the heat but lower it to medium.

Add the shallots and remaining 2 tablespoons of olive oil and sauté for 5 minutes, until translucent. Add the garlic, cremini and portobello mushrooms, and thyme. Sauté for about 10 minutes, until the mushrooms have browned slightly and released their moisture.

In the meantime, prepare a 4-quart pot with lightly salted water for the pasta. Cover and bring to a boil. Once boiling, add the pasta and cook according to the package directions.

Back to the sauce. Add the salt, wine, and paprika to the mushroom mixture. Turn up the heat to high to reduce the liquid, about 10 minutes.

Add the cornstarch mixture, stir well, and let the sauce thicken, about 7 minutes. Add the nutritional yeast, milk, and mustard. Mix well and lower the heat to low; be very careful not to let it boil now because it could make the milk and mustard bitter. Add the seitan and peas; cook for 5 more minutes.

The pasta should be done by now. Divide the noodles among bowls and top with the stroganoff. It is best to serve immediately so that the pasta doesn't stick. Garnish with fresh parsley, if you like!

COLD UDON NOODLES WITH PEANUT SAUCE AND SEITAN

SERVES 4 TO 6

FOR THE PEANUT SAUCE:

2 teaspoons olive oil

2 cloves minced garlic

2 tablespoons minced fresh ginger

2 teaspoons coriander seeds, crushed (see Fizzle says, page 17)

2 tablespoons soy sauce

⅔ cup smooth all-natural peanut butter

2 tablespoons agave nectar

3 tablespoons rice vinegar

1 tablespoon sriracha (or more or less to taste)

FOR THE NOODLES AND SEITAN:

10 ounces udon noodles

2 cups seitan (page 170), sliced into ¼-inch-thick strips

1 tablespoon olive oil

1 clove garlic, minced

2 teaspoons soy sauce

TO SERVE:

¼ cup black sesame seeds (optional)

1 seedless cucumber, halved across, sliced into matchsticks

4 cups bean sprouts

1 red bell pepper, thinly sliced

2 cups chopped scallions

Several lime wedges for serving

I crave peanut noodles like nobody's business. I came up with this recipe over twenty years ago and still use it today! Temperature is important. The noodles and vegetables should be cold as can be, the sauce should be at room temperature, and the seitan should be warm. If you follow the directions, you should have no problemo getting it all right. If you aren't serving immediately and the peanut sauce has been refrigerated, let the sauce sit out until it reaches room temperature.

To make the peanut sauce: In a small saucepan, sauté the garlic, ginger, and coriander seed in the olive oil over medium-low heat for about a minute. Add 1 cup of water and soy sauce and bring to a boil. Add the peanut butter and turn the heat to low. Whisk well until the peanut butter is well combined. Mix in the agave, vinegar, and sriracha. Remove from the heat and let cool to room temperature.

Meanwhile, make the noodles and seitan: Prepare your udon noodles according to the package directions. When noodles have cooked, drain them in a colander and rinse them under cold water until they are cool to the touch. Let them rest in the colander and prepare the seitan.

Sauté the seitan slices in the olive oil over medium heat for 5 minutes, until browned and yummy. Then sauté with the garlic for a minute, sprinkle with the soy sauce, and sauté again for 30 seconds or so.

At this point, your peanut sauce should be at room temperature. Give the noodles a final rinse under cold water to make them cold and also to keep them from sticking together.

To serve, place the noodles on a large platter. Pour the peanut sauce over the noodles, then sprinkle with the sesame seeds, if using. Scatter the cucumber, bean sprouts, and pepper on top, followed by the scallions. Place the warm seitan on top and place lime wedges around the circumference and, gosh darn it, you've got yourself a fine-looking meal. If you prefer to serve on individual plates to keep the greedy people from stealing all the seitan, then just follow the directions but divide everything among four to six plates.

ETHIOPIAN SEITAN AND PEPPERS

FOR THE PUREE:

4 serrano chiles, seeded
and coarsely chopped
(see Fizzle says, page 62)

1 tablespoon chopped fresh ginger

2 cloves garlic, crushed

1 teaspoon ground cumin

¼ teaspoon ground cardamom

¼ teaspoon ground turmeric

¼ teaspoon ground cloves

¼ teaspoon ground cinnamon

½ cup red wine

3 tablespoons olive oil

FOR THE SEITAN AND PEPPERS:

4 cups seitan (page 170), sliced into
¼-inch-thick slices

2 green bell peppers, seeded and
cut into ½-inch strips

Oh goodness, there is some amazing vegan Ethiopian food all over the USA. From Philly to Portland, you can find me with a big platter of it, trying to hog the whole thing but pretending that I enjoy sharing with my friends. Anyway, I remember finding an Ethiopian cookbook in the library many, many years ago, and I believe that is where I modified this recipe from. It is really spicy and complex, with an underlying and unmistakable clove essence that I always inhale the moment I step into an Ethiopian restaurant.

Preheat the oven to 400°F.

Place all the puree ingredients in a blender and puree until relatively smooth.

Place the seitan strips and peppers in a 9 x 13-inch baking dish; smother with the puree. Cover with foil and bake for 20 minutes. Remove the foil, flip the seitan and peppers, and cook for 20 more minutes. Serve with rice and green vegetables.

KABOCHA SQUASH STUFFED
with BUTTERNUT VINDALOO

MAKES 6 STUFFED SQUASHES

3 tablespoons peanut oil

2 cups diced yellow onion

3 cloves garlic, minced

2 tablespoons grated fresh ginger

1 tablespoon mustard seeds

1 tablespoon ground cumin

½ teaspoon ground cloves

4 cardamom pods

2 cinnamon sticks

¼ cup red wine vinegar

½ cup red wine

1 (12-ounce) can crushed tomatoes

1½ pounds Yukon gold potatoes, peeled and cut into ½-inch chunks

1½ pounds butternut squash, cut into ½-inch chunks

6 medium-size kabocha squashes

¼ cup pure maple syrup

Chopped fresh cilantro for garnish

Vindaloo is a spicy sweet-and-sour curry. Naturally sweet winter squash, both in the stew and when serving in a bowl, tastes great in this and mellows out the spiciness. If you don't feel like baking the kabocha squash to stuff, then simply serve the butternut vindaloo over some basmati rice.

In a 4-quart pot over medium heat, sauté the onion in the peanut oil for 5 to 7 minutes. Add the garlic and ginger; sauté until fragrant (about a minute); add all the seeds and spices and stir. Let them cook for about 2 minutes. Mix in the red wine vinegar, red wine, and tomatoes. Add the potatoes and butternut squash, cover, and bring to a low boil. Cook until the potatoes are tender, about 25 minutes.

Meanwhile, prepare the kabocha squashes: Preheat the oven to 375°F. Lightly grease a rimmed baking sheet. Cut off the top of the kabocha squashes and remove the seeds. Scrape inside with a tablespoon to remove the stringy parts. Cut a small sliver off the bottom of each squash so that you will later be able to stand the squash upright to stuff it. Place the squashes, cut side down, on the baking sheet, and bake for about 40 minutes. The squashes should be very soft and easily pierced with a fork.

Back to the stew: When the potatoes are tender, add the maple syrup and heat through. Cover and keep warm until the squashes are ready.

Remove the squash from the oven and, when cool enough to handle, stuff each with some of the stew. Garnish with cilantro and serve.

176 VEGAN WITH A VENGEANCE

LEMONGRASS NOODLE BOWL
with MOCK DUCK

MARINATED SEITAN:

¼ cup chopped shallot

1 clove garlic

1 teaspoon agave nectar

A few dashes of freshly ground black pepper

1 tablespoon soy sauce

1 tablespoon peanut oil (or canola oil)

2 tablespoons sliced lemongrass (see Fizzle says, page 182)

Juice of 1 lime

2 cups thinly sliced seitan (page 170)

BROTH:

2 tablespoons coriander seeds

1 tablespoon peanut oil (or canola oil)

1 (2-inch) nub fresh ginger, thinly sliced (no need to peel)

6 cloves garlic, smashed

1 large white onion, roughly chopped

3 tablespoons sliced lemongrass (see Fizzle says, page 182)

1 teaspoon salt

4 cups vegan vegetable broth (or equivalent bouillon)

Juice of 1 lime

TO SERVE:

8 ounces vermicelli rice noodles

Sriracha

Thinly sliced red onion

Thinly sliced red pepper

Lots of fresh mint

Lots of fresh cilantro

Lime wedges

This dish is bursting with crave-worthy Vietnamese flavors: lemongrass, lime, mint, ginger . . . if matzoh ball soup is Jewish penicillin, then this noodle bowl is a flu shot. I like to use homemade broth and infuse it with aromatics, but you can use bouillon, if you like. Just try not to make the base too strong; you want all the flavors to shine through.

Mock duck is really just seitan, but if you're familiar with those little cans of "mock duck" at the Asian grocery, feel free to use those!

First, marinate the seitan: Toss all the marinade ingredients, except the seitan, into a small food processor and puree until (relatively) smooth.

Place the seitan in the marinade. Let marinate for about an hour, turning a couple of times to keep everything evenly coated.

CONTINUED >>>

>>> CONTINUED FROM PAGE 177

Meanwhile, prepare the broth: Heat a stockpot over medium heat. Dry toast the coriander seeds for about 3 minutes, until they're fragrant and a few shades darker. Add the peanut oil, onion, garlic, and ginger and sauté for about 15 minutes. Add the lemongrass, salt, broth, and 6 cups of water. Cover and bring to a boil. Once boiling, lower to a simmer and cook for about 30 more minutes, or until everything else is ready.

While the broth is simmering, prepare your noodles according to the package directions. Once they are ready, drain and rinse under cold water and set aside. It's okay if they're at room temp.

Then prepare the mock duck: Heat a large pan (preferably cast iron) over medium heat. Drizzle a little peanut oil in the pan. Sauté the mock duck for about 10 minutes, until nicely browned. Oh, and if you like things spicy, add a big pinch of red pepper flakes while sautéing.

Back to the broth. After it has simmered for 30 minutes or after all other components are ready, strain the broth through a fine-mesh strainer (remember to have a large bowl underneath, obviously), then return to the pot to keep warm. Add the lime juice.

To assemble the bowls, place one quarter of the noodles in each of four large bowls. Pour in the broth. Add sriracha to taste. Tuck the veggies and fresh herbs all over. Top with the mock duck and garnish with lime wedges. Serve with a fork or chopsticks and a large spoon.

1 (12-ounce) can whole tomatoes (in juice, not puree)

3 tablespoons vegetable oil

2 teaspoons mustard seeds

1 large onion, cut into ¼-inch dice (about 2 cups)

4 cloves garlic, minced

2 tablespoons minced fresh ginger

3 teaspoons curry powder

2 teaspoons ground cumin

1 teaspoon ground coriander

⅛ teaspoon ground cloves

½ teaspoon ground cinnamon

¼ teaspoon asafoetida (optional)

3 cardamom pods

1 teaspoon salt

10 cups fresh spinach, well rinsed and chopped

4 cups chickpeas, cooked and drained (or 2 [15-ounce] cans, drained and rinsed

I pretty much live on curries. I can't think of any other dish that packs so much flavor with so little work. I love tomato-based curries; here the tomatoes are a pleasant backdrop and a sturdy base that isn't screaming tomato, so the spices can really shine through. It doesn't hurt that a tomato base has considerably less fat than, say, coconut milk, if you care about that sort of thing. Make sure your mustard seeds are visibly popping before adding the onion; if you've never cooked your own mustard seeds before, you're in for a treat that will change your curry making for good.

Prepare the tomatoes by removing them one at a time from the can, squeezing out the juice, and tearing them into bite-size pieces. Place the prepared tomatoes in a bowl and reserve the juice in the can.

Heat a medium-size saucepan over medium heat; pour in the vegetable oil and then the mustard seeds. Let the seeds pop for about a minute (you may want to cover the pot so that the seeds can't escape), then add the onion. Turn up the heat to medium-high and sauté for 7 to 10 minutes, until the onion begins to brown. Add the garlic and ginger and sauté for 2 more minutes. Add the spices, salt, and ¼ cup of the reserved tomato juice; sauté for 1 minute more. Add the tomatoes and heat through. Add handfuls of spinach, mixing each addition, until wilted. When all the spinach has completely wilted and the mixture is liquidy, add the chickpeas. Lower the heat, cover, and simmer for 10 more minutes, stirring occasionally. Taste, and adjust the spices, if necessary. Simmer, uncovered, for about 10 more minutes, or until a thick, stewlike consistency is achieved.

Fizzle says:

Asafoetida, also called hing powder, is a root resin used in small doses in many Indian dishes. It's a little hard to find; you may need to go to a spice store, so it is optional in this recipe. If you can find it, though, you will fall in love with its aromatic scent and flavor.

GREEN THAI CURRY

FOR THE CHILE PASTE:

2 small Thai green peppers or serrano chiles, seeded and chopped (see Fizzle says, page 62)

2 jalapeño peppers, seeded and chopped (see Fizzle says, page 62)

½ cup boiling water

2 teaspoons crushed coriander seeds

1 teaspoon cumin seeds

5 white peppercorns (black peppercorns are an okay substitution)

1 tablespoon chopped fresh lemongrass (see Fizzle says, page 182)

1 tablespoon chopped fresh ginger (or galangal if you can find it)

3 cloves garlic

1 cup lightly packed fresh cilantro

2 teaspoons finely grated lime zest

1 cup chopped shallots

EVERYTHING ELSE:

5 tablespoons peanut oil

1 (12-ounce) block tofu, pressed and cut into small triangles (page 158)

1 red bell pepper, seeded and thinly sliced

1 medium-size red onion, sliced into thin half-moons

1 (15-ounce) can coconut milk

1½ tablespoons pure maple syrup

Juice of 1 lime

½ cup lightly packed fresh basil (Thai basil if you can find it)

Fresh cilantro for garnish

Making your own chile paste is easy and flavorful. While admittedly you won't be saving money by not purchasing the chile paste in a jar, you will embark on a culinary adventure that makes it worth it: the taste of homemade chile paste is just incomparable. There are several steps here, but you should be able to have dinner on the table within an hour, provided your tofu is already pressed. This is a great dish to serve a date, alongside the Fresh Mango Summer Rolls (page 89) and some jasmine rice.

TO PREPARE THE CHILE PASTE:

Place the serranos and jalapeños in a bowl, cover with a ½ cup of boiling water, and let sit for 15 minutes.

Place the coriander seeds, cumin seeds, and peppercorns in a small skillet and toast over medium heat for about 2 minutes, until they are fragrant. Transfer to a food processor and grind into a powder. (If you

CONTINUED ⟩⟩⟩

are using a blender instead, it may not grind the seeds into a powder, it may just bounce them around, so either use a mortar and pestle or a coffee grinder to grind them or just place them with all the other ingredients and hope for the best.) Add the remaining ingredients, including the chiles in their water; grind to a paste. Cover and set aside until ready to use.

TO MAKE EVERYTHING ELSE:

Heat 2 tablespoons of the peanut oil in a large, nonstick skillet over medium-high heat. Add the tofu triangles and heat on each side until golden brown (about 4 minutes per side). Transfer to a large plate and cover with foil to keep warm. In the same skillet, sauté the red pepper and onion (add a little extra oil, if needed) for about 3 minutes, until just slightly tender.

Heat a medium-size, heavy-bottomed saucepan over medium-low heat. Add the chile paste and cook for about 2 minutes, stirring constantly. Add the coconut milk and turn up the heat a bit. Mix together until the paste is incorporated; bring to a low boil. Add the maple syrup and lime juice, taste for sweetness, then add a little more maple syrup, if necessary. Place the tofu mixture in the sauce and cover; cook for 5 minutes. Add the basil and turn off the heat. Let sit for 5 minutes or so before serving. Transfer to serving bowls and garnish with fresh cilantro.

 *Fizzle says:*

Lemongrass looks sort of like a long stalk of bamboo but the only part you actually use is the heart of the stalk. You'll have to cut off and discard the rest where the leaves start to branch and then peel off the rough outer leaves. The remaining "heart" can then be diced with a sharp knife.

BLACK-EYED PEA CURRY
with COLLARDS AND POTATOES

1 tablespoon refined coconut oil

1 large red onion, thinly sliced

2 jalapeño peppers, seeded and thinly sliced (see Fizzle says, page 62)

2 cloves garlic, minced

1 tablespoon minced fresh ginger

1½ to 2 tablespoons mild curry powder

½ teaspoon garam masala

¾ teaspoon salt

3 cups vegan vegetable broth

1 tablespoon agave nectar

2 tablespoons tomato paste

1½ pounds red potatoes, cut into ¾-inch pieces

1 pound collards, rough stems removed, leaves chopped into bite-size pieces

1½ cups cooked black eyed peas (from a 15-ounce, drained and rinsed)

1 cup coconut milk

FOR THE MANGO-AVOCADO SALSA:

1 ripe avocado, diced

1 ripe mango, diced

1 tablespoon freshly squeezed lime juice

Chopped fresh cilantro for garnish (optional)

Chunky red potatoes, velvety collards, and earthy black-eyed peas make for a voluptuous coconut curry that is slightly out of the ordinary. It comes together real fast, too. The sauce creates a verrrry versatile and basic curry. You can swap out the black-eyed peas for chickpeas, or the greens for spinach or kale. You can even swap out the red potatoes for sweet potatoes (keeping in mind that sweet potatoes cook a lot faster.) Don't replace the tomato paste with ketchup or the coconut milk with orange juice or anything gross like that. Serve with basmati rice and Mango-Avocado Salsa for sweetness, tartness, and a little extra creaminess. Have some sriracha at the ready in case you want a little extra spice!

Heat a 4-quart pot over medium heat. Sauté the onion and jalapeño in the coconut oil for 5 to 7 minutes, until the onion is lightly browned.

Add the garlic and ginger, and sauté until fragrant, about 30 seconds. Add 1½ tablespoons of curry powder and the garam masala, salt, broth, agave, and tomato paste; stir. The tomato paste may not dissolve just yet but that's okay; it will when it heats through.

Add the potatoes, cover the pot, and bring to a boil. Once boiling, immediately lower the heat to a simmer, and leave the lid ajar so that steam can escape. Let the potatoes cook just until tender, about 5 more minutes.

Prepare the salsa: In the meantime, toss together all the salsa ingredients in a mixing bowl and set aside.

Once the potatoes are fork tender, add the collards, black-eyed peas, and coconut milk and stir gently to incorporate. Re-cover, leaving the lid ajar again, and bring to a simmer. Let simmer just until the collards are tender; it should only take a few minutes.

Turn off the heat and taste for salt and spices. Add the remaining curry powder, if needed. The curry tastes best if you let it sit for 10 minutes or so to let the flavors mingle, but if you can't wait, then just dig in! Serve over basmati rice, topped with mango avocado salsa and cilantro, if you like.

RUSTIC LENTIL STEW over POLENTA

FOR THE STEW:

2 tablespoons olive oil

1 small yellow onion, diced medium

2 cloves garlic, minced

1 teaspoon dried thyme

½ teaspoon celery seeds

A few dashes of freshly ground black pepper

1 teaspoon salt

½ cup dried green lentils

1½ cups baby carrots

2 pounds plum tomatoes, chopped

4 cups vegan vegetable broth

1 pound small Yukon gold potatoes, sliced in half (if using large ones, cut into about 1-inch pieces)

2 bay leaves

3 leeks, white and light green parts only, cut into 1-inch chunks (and washed well)

Fresh rosemary or thyme, to serve (realistically, only if you're taking food photos)

FOR THE POLENTA:

4 cups vegan vegetable broth

½ teaspoon salt

2 tablespoons olive oil

1 cup dried polenta

love that the addition of one word can turn a sloppy one-pot meal into something refined. The word, of course, being *rustic*. This is a hit-the-spot stew for wintertime, and the addition of a soft, simple, and creamy polenta make it pure comfort. (Of course, if you don't want to use polenta, you can use mashed potatoes, rice, or any manner of yummy starches.) The lentils add extra body and some meatiness to the dish. And, for easy prep, choose smaller Yukon gold potatoes that are about the size of a misshapen golf ball—that way, you only need to slice them in half to prep.

TO MAKE THE STEW:

Heat a 4-quart pot over medium heat. Sauté the onion in olive oil, along with a dash of salt, for about 5 minutes. Add the garlic, thyme, celery seeds, pepper and salt and sauté for a minute more until fragrant.

Add the lentils, baby carrots, tomatoes, and broth. Cover pot and bring to a boil. Stir occasionally for about 20 minutes, until lentils are slightly softened.

While the stew simmers, prepare the polenta. Bring the broth and salt to a boil in a 2-quart pot. Add the olive oil and lower the heat to a simmer. Add the polenta in a slow, steady stream, stirring constantly with a whisk. Whisk for about 5 minutes, until the polenta is thickened. Keeping the heat low, cover and let cook for 20 more minutes or so, stirring occasionally.

Once the polenta is going, return to the stew and add the potatoes, bay leaves, and leeks. Lower the heat to a simmer. Cover and cook for 20 to 30 more minutes, until the potatoes are fork tender and the lentils are soft. Let sit for 10 minutes or so to allow the flavors to meld. Remove the bay leaves before serving. Serve over the polenta, garnished with fresh herbs, if you like.

SWEET POTATO CREPES WITH CILANTRO-TAMARIND SAUCE

1 recipe Savory Crepes
(page 187)

FOR THE SPICE BLEND:

2 teaspoons cumin seeds

1 teaspoon coriander seeds

1 teaspoon fenugreek seeds

1 teaspoon mustard seeds

2 cardamom pods

6 whole cloves

Pinch of ground cinnamon

Pinch of ground cayenne pepper

½ teaspoon salt

FOR THE FILLING:

2 tablespoons peanut oil

1½ cups finely chopped yellow
onion

1 red bell pepper, finely chopped

2 cloves garlic, minced

2 tablespoons grated fresh ginger

2½ pounds sweet potatoes, peeled
and chopped into ½-inch chunks

½ (15-ounce) can coconut milk

1 tablespoon pure maple syrup

1 tablespoon freshly squeezed
lime juice

FOR THE SAUCE:

½ cup raw cashews

2 cups lightly packed fresh cilantro,
plus extra for garnish

2 teaspoons tamarind concentrate

¾ cup coconut milk

1 teaspoon agave nectar (or sugar)

Pinch of salt

The slightly sweet and aromatic filling wrapped in a warm crepe and smothered in a rich yet delicate sauce is sure to impress. We toasted our own spices to bring extra-fresh flavor to the curried sweet potatoes, but if you don't want to go the extra mile, even though you really should, then you can use ground spices.

Prepare the spice blend: Heat a small skillet over medium heat. Scatter in all the seeds, pods, and the cloves (do not add the cinnamon and cayenne now), and toast for about 3 minutes, shaking the skillet back and forth for even heating. The spices should smell warm and toasty. Remove the mixture from the pan immediately and transfer to a bowl to cool. When fully cooled, place in a spice grinder (a coffee grinder works) and grind to a fine powder, then add the cinnamon, cayenne, and salt. Set aside.

Prepare the filling: Heat a large skillet over medium heat. Sauté the onion and bell pepper in oil with a pinch of salt for about 5 minutes. Add the garlic and ginger; sauté for about 2 minutes more. Add the spice blend and make sure the onion is coated with it. Add the sweet potatoes and cook for a minute or two. Cover the pan and cook for 15 more minutes, stirring frequently, until the sweet potatoes are tender. (You should prepare the sauce while they are cooking.) Add the coconut milk, maple syrup, and lime juice, cover, and cook for 5 more minutes, stirring occasionally. The coconut milk should be fully incorporated into the sweet potatoes.

While the filling cooks, prepare the sauce: Grind the cashews in a blender or food processor. Add the remaining ingredients and blend until relatively smooth. That's it!

Place one crepe on a plate, fill with about ½ cup of filling and fold each side over, like a jacket. Repeat with a second crepe and drizzle with sauce. Continue with the remaining crepes, filling, and sauce. There should be two crepes per plate. Garnish with cilantro and serve!

SAVORY CREPES

1½ cups all-purpose flour

½ cup chickpea flour

1 teaspoon salt

2 tablespoons olive oil

This is Terry's recipe from when she worked in an '80s vegan restaurant. The chickpea flour adds hints of egginess. Don't worry if your first crepe isn't perfect; even pros tear a crepe or two from time to time. Just move on to the next one.

Combine the flours and salt in a medium-size mixing bowl. Make a well in the center of the flour mixture and add 2 cups of water and the olive oil. Use an electric hand mixer to blend until completely smooth (if you don't have a mixer, mix with a fork for a good solid 3 minutes). Cover the batter with plastic wrap and let chill in the fridge for ½ hour or so.

Heat your crepe pan or a nonstick skillet that is 8 inches or so across. Spray the pan with nonstick cooking spray or a very thin layer of olive oil. Pour ¼ cup of batter into the pan; tilt and rotate the pan so that the crepe batter has covered the bottom and crept up the sides of the pan just a tiny bit. When it looks like the top of the crepe has pretty much set and the corners of the crepes are just beginning to brown, flip over with a spatula and cook the other side for just under a minute.

You can remove the crepe in one of two ways (and probably more than two but this is how I do it): (1) fold the crepe in half and then in half again, so that it's folded into a triangular shape; or (2) use a spatula to transfer the crepe to a large plate, putting a sheet of waxed paper between each crepe to keep them from sticking. You may be able to get away with not using the waxed paper if you'd like to chance it. Either way you do it, cover the plate with foil as you make the remainder of the crepes.

BROOKLYN PAD THAI

1 pound rice noodles

FOR THE SAUCE:

6 tablespoons tamari

6 tablespoons sugar

2 tablespoons tomato paste

2 tablespoons sriracha

¼ cup rice wine vinegar

3 tablespoons tamarind concentrate or freshly squeezed lime juice

FOR THE PAD THAI:

3 tablespoons peanut oil

14 ounces extra-firm tofu, drained and cubed

1 medium-size red onion, cut into thin half-moons

2 cloves garlic, minced

1 tablespoon finely minced lemongrass (see Fizzle says, page 182)

2 cups bean sprouts

8 scallions, sliced into 1½-inch lengths

2 small dried red chiles, crumbled

½ cup chopped roasted peanuts

¼ cup chopped fresh cilantro

Lime wedges for serving

Is this authentic? Most assuredly not, but it does taste a lot like the pad thai served every two feet in Brooklyn. It's spicy, savory, sweet, and sour—exactly what you want in pad thai!

This makes enough to serve four people. I originally suggested making this recipe two servings at a time, but if you have a big-ass gigantic wok, you can make it all at once. Otherwise, I suggest dividing the ingredients in half for two cooking sessions, so that the noodles don't become mushy.

Prepare the rice noodles according to the package directions. Run them under cold water to cool completely.

Mix together the ingredients for the sauce.

Begin cooking the pad thai: Heat a large, nonstick skillet or wok over medium-high heat. Pour 2 tablespoons of the peanut oil into the pan and heat, then quickly add the tofu. Stir-fry for 4 to 5 minutes, until the tofu is crisp on the outside. Remove from pan and set aside.

Pour the remaining tablespoon of peanut oil into the pan and sauté the red onion for about 2 minutes. Add the garlic and lemongrass, and stir-fry for 30 more seconds. Add the sauce and, when it starts to bubble (should bubble within a few seconds), add the noodles. Cook for 2 minutes, stirring constantly, then add the tofu, bean sprouts, scallions, and chiles. Stir for 30 more seconds. Transfer to serving plates and garnish with peanuts, cilantro, and lime wedges.

1 cup millet

3 cups vegan vegetable broth

1 tablespoon olive oil, plus extra for cooking the polenta

2 cups shredded fresh spinach, well rinsed

1 tablespoon chopped fresh oregano

½ teaspoon salt

A few dashes of freshly ground black pepper

Sun-dried Tomato Pesto (recipe follows)

I got the idea for millet polenta from a fabulous book called *The Splendid Grain*. It's kind of hippie and wholesome and I don't really care. It's easier to prepare than polenta made with the traditional cornmeal because it doesn't require as much stirring and attention. This is a yummy version, flecked with spinach and oregano and topped with a savory Sun-dried Tomato Pesto. Toasting the millet beforehand brings out its nutty flavor.

Toast the millet in a dry skillet for about 5 minutes over high heat, stirring constantly, until the millet releases a nutty aroma. Rinse in a fine-mesh sieve or a large bowl, until the water runs clear; drain as best you can.

Bring the millet, broth, and olive oil to a boil in a saucepan. Lower the heat and simmer for about 25 minutes. Mix in the spinach, oregano, salt, and pepper; simmer for 10 more minutes, uncovered, until all the liquid is absorbed.

You have a few options for molding your polenta; it all depends on the shape that you want.

FOR SQUARES OR RECTANGLES:

Lightly grease a lidded plastic container that is roughly 11 x 7 inches. Spread the polenta into the container and let cool on the countertop. When fully cooled, cut into your desired size of rectangles.

FOR CIRCLES:

Lightly grease two 16-ounce tin cans or three 12-ounce juice concentrate containers. Spoon the polenta into the containers and pack tightly; let cool on the countertop. When fully cooled, remove the polenta from the containers and cut into 1-inch slices. Note: It may take up to 2 hours for the polenta to get firm enough to cool in the cans. If you try to remove it before then, it will break and you will be sad. You may also need to drag a thin knife around the circumference to loosen the polenta. The juice concentrate containers are a great deal easier to unmold: you can jiggle them upside down until the polenta loosens and comes out. If it won't budge, rip or cut the edge of the container with scissors and unravel it as necessary.

PREPARE THE POLENTA:

Heat a large skillet over medium heat for a minute or two. Coat the pan with a very thin layer of olive oil; fry the polenta on each side for 3 minutes. Serve immediately, topped with Sun-dried Tomato Pesto, and with roasted asparagus on the side.

SUN-DRIED TOMATO PESTO

MAKES ABOUT 1½ CUPS

½ cup tightly packed sun-dried tomatoes (not oil-packed)

¼ cup almonds

2 cloves garlic, chopped

2 tablespoons olive oil

¼ teaspoon salt

A few dashes of freshly ground black pepper

¼ cup chopped fresh basil

Place the sun-dried tomatoes in a saucepan and cover with 1 cup of water. Bring to a low boil, then turn off the heat and let soak for about 15 minutes, until soft.

Grind the almonds in a blender or food processor. Add the sun-dried tomatoes (with the water), garlic, olive oil, salt, and pepper, and puree.

Transfer to a bowl and stir in the basil. Let sit for a few minutes to allow the flavors to blend.

REVOLUTIONARY SPANISH OMELET WITH SAFFRON AND ROASTED RED PEPPER–ALMOND SAUCE

A small pinch of saffron threads

3 tablespoons boiling water

¼ cup plus 1 tablespoon olive oil, plus extra for spraying omelet

4 medium-size unpeeled Yukon gold potatoes, halved and sliced into ¼-inch slices (make sure they're all the same thickness, to ensure even cooking)

1 medium-size onion, sliced into thin half-moons

1½ pounds soft tofu, drained

2 cloves garlic, crushed

1 teaspoon salt

Dash of cayenne pepper

This is another wonderful recipe from Terry Hope Romero, and even though it's an omelet, it makes a great entrée. She tells us, "If the anarchist revolutionaries in the Spanish Civil War had known about the magic of tofu, they would have made a traditional dish just like this. Or maybe it's just my hopes for an egalitarian, nonauthoritarian society talking again. Known in Spain simply as a 'tortilla,' the thick, oven-baked omelet of eggs, potatoes, onions, and olive oil is found in virtually every café and can be eaten at any meal any time of day. Below is a liberatingly egg-free version—with the addition of saffron—that bakes up a beautiful golden yellow with the delicate flavor of the classic Spanish spice. The flavors improve with time so you can make it the night before and serve cold or at room temperature. Along with a dollop of Roasted Red Pepper–Almond Sauce (page 194) and crusty bread, this tortilla of the Revolution is a sturdy meal that will carry you through many an anarcho-syndicalist collective workers' meeting."

Place the saffron threads in a small cup and gently press the threads with the back of a spoon a few times; don't crush completely. Pour the boiling water over the saffron; stir briefly, then set aside for a minimum of 25 minutes. The longer the saffron soaks, the more flavor and color will be released.

Preheat the oven to 375°F. Pour ¼ cup of the olive oil into a 10-inch cast-iron skillet. Add the potatoes and onion. The pan should not be completely full; there should be about ¼ inch of space left on top; remove some potatoes if it appears too full. Gently toss the onion and potatoes in the oil to coat. Place in the oven and roast for 30 to 35 minutes, stirring on occasion, until the onion is very soft and the potatoes are tender.

Meanwhile, in a food processor, blend until smooth the drained tofu, garlic, and remaining 1 tablespoon of olive oil. Strain the saffron with a fine-mesh strainer and add the liquid to the tofu mixture along with salt and cayenne pepper. Blend until creamy.

CONTINUED >>>

When the potato mixture is tender, remove from the oven. Pour the tofu mixture into the pan and gently fold the potato mixture into the tofu mixture. With a rubber spatula, smooth the top, making sure to make the center slightly more shallow than the outside; this will help ensure the center cooks evenly.

Spray the top of the omelet with olive oil and return to the oven. Bake for 50 minutes to 1 hour, until the top is deep yellow and lightly browned in spots, and a knife inserted into the center comes out clean. Remove from the oven and allow to cool for at least 20 minutes before cutting.

To cut, run a knife along the edges, pressing down on the omelet while slicing. To serve it real Spanish style you'll need to remove it whole from the pan: put a plate on top of the pan and, with both hands securely holding pan and plate, flip the entire thing upside down. Put on a countertop and gently remove the pan—the finished omelet is oily enough so most of it should slide easily onto the plate. If you preferred the golden yellow side to be on top, simply flip again onto another plate.

Excellent both warm and at room temperature. Serve as the Spanish do with ketchup (a good all-natural one worthy of revolutionaries) or with Roasted Red Pepper–Almond Sauce.

ROASTED RED PEPPER–ALMOND SAUCE

MAKES ABOUT 1¼ CUPS

3 roasted red peppers (homemade or equivalent amount from a jar)

¼ cup slivered almonds

2 cloves garlic, peeled and crushed

3 tablespoons olive oil

¼ cup freshly squeezed lemon juice

1 teaspoon dried thyme

1½ teaspoons sugar

Salt

Blend all the ingredients, including salt to taste, in a food processor until thick and creamy.

MOROCCAN TAGINE
with SPRING VEGETABLES

2 tablespoons olive oil

2 medium-size onions, quartered and thinly sliced

1 cup small-diced carrot

1 serrano chile, seeded and minced (see Fizzle says, page 62)

3 cloves garlic, minced

2 tablespoons grated fresh ginger

2 teaspoons ground cumin

1 teaspoon ground turmeric

1 teaspoon ground coriander

4 cups vegan vegetable broth

2 tablespoons tomato paste

2 cinnamon sticks

2 bay leaves

A few dashes of freshly ground black pepper

1 cup dried red lentils, washed

1 zucchini, halved lengthwise and sliced ¼ inch thick

1 cup green beans, cut into 1-inch pieces

2 cups grape tomatoes, halved

½ cup raisins

1 teaspoon salt

1 bunch spinach, torn into pieces (4 cups)

½ cup chopped fresh cilantro leaves

½ cup chopped fresh mint

Lemon wedges to serve

Tagine is the name of the traditional clay pot used by Moroccans to produce flavorful and aromatic stews and other dishes. The name was carried over in America to include stews made with spices often used in Moroccan cooking. Or so they tell me. This is a deliciously spiced stew that I'm sure they don't actually serve in Morocco, but what the hell. The ingredients list looks *long*. That's because it is. But really, it's just because there's a lot of yummy spices. The recipe itself isn't difficult, so don't be intimidated. It's packed full of vegetables and lentils, making this tagine a veritable powerhouse of nutrition. Serve over couscous.

Heat a 4-quart pot over medium-heat. Sauté the onions in the olive oil for 3 minutes. Add the carrots and chile and sauté for 3 minutes more. Add the garlic and ginger; sauté for 2 minutes. Add the cumin, turmeric, and coriander, and mix. Add the broth, tomato paste, cinnamon sticks, bay leaves, black pepper, and lentils. Bring to a boil, then lower the heat and simmer, uncovered, for 20 minutes, or until the lentils are tender.

Add the zucchini, green beans, tomatoes, except the spinach, and the raisins and salt, then simmer for 15 more minutes. Add the spinach, cilantro, and mint and stir well. When the spinach has wilted completely, about 1 minute, turn off the heat. Let the stew sit for 10 minutes for the flavors to marry. Remove the bay leaves and cinnamon sticks. Thin with extra broth or water, if necessary. Serve with lemon wedges for squeezing in.

MUSHROOM AND SUN-DRIED TOMATO RISOTTO

6 cups vegan vegetable broth

1 cup dried shiitake mushrooms

3 tablespoons olive oil

1 cup finely chopped shallots

3 cups thinly sliced cremini mushrooms

¼ cup chopped sun-dried tomatoes

2 garlic cloves, minced

1 tablespoon minced fresh thyme

2 teaspoons minced fresh rosemary

½ teaspoon ground or freshly grated nutmeg

A few dashes of freshly ground black pepper

½ teaspoon salt

1½ cups arborio rice

A few drops of black truffle oil (optional)

Risotto is a creamy rice dish that isn't difficult to make but does require a lot of maintenance; you need to stir it pretty much constantly. Try to get your roommates or family to help with the stirring, although when I make it alone, I just blast some music and go into a Zen-like trance, where it's just the risotto and me on a hillside in Italy. I added truffle oil as an optional ingredient because it can cost about $10 a bottle, but you need only a few drops to add a deep, earthy mushroom flavor and that bottle can definitely last you a year or more; compared to the price of actual truffles, that's quite a bargain.

Bring the broth to a simmer in a medium-size saucepan. Add the dried shiitake mushrooms and simmer for about 2 minutes, until the mushrooms are tender. Using a slotted spoon, transfer the mushrooms to a plate. When cool enough to handle, coarsely chop them. Cover the broth and keep warm over very low heat.

In a medium-size saucepan over medium heat, sauté the shallots in the olive oil for about 5 minutes; add the cremini mushrooms and sun-dried tomatoes, and cook until the mushrooms are tender and most of the moisture has been released, about 7 minutes. Add the garlic, chopped shiitakes, herbs, nutmeg, and salt; sauté another 3 minutes.

Add the rice and stir with a wooden spoon for 2 minutes. Add 1 cup of broth; stirring often, simmer until the liquid is absorbed, about 6 minutes. Continue to cook and stir, adding more broth by the cupful, until the rice is tender and creamy and all the broth is absorbed. This should take about 30 minutes. Spoon onto plates and sprinkle some truffle oil over each serving, if you like.

EGGPLANT AND ARTICHOKE ALLA NAPOLETANA

FOR THE ARTICHOKE FILLING:

3 tablespoons extra-virgin olive oil

1 small yellow onion, finely chopped

2 garlic cloves, minced

½ teaspoon dried thyme

½ teaspoon salt

A few dashes of freshly ground black pepper

8 plum tomatoes, diced

2 cups coarsely chopped artichoke hearts (if using canned, be sure to wash off any seasoning)

½ cup thinly sliced, pitted kalamata olives

¼ cup capers, drained

¼ cup chopped fresh basil

FOR THE EGGPLANT SLICES:

1 tablespoon organic cornstarch

1 cup all-purpose flour

1 cup panko

¼ teaspoon dried thyme

¼ teaspoon dried oregano

½ teaspoon salt

A few dashes of freshly ground black pepper

Oil for frying

1 large eggplant, sliced ¼ inch thick

Sauce of your choice, such as Pizza Sauce (page 138) or one of the pestos (pages 137, 191)

This is bread crumb–coated eggplant layered with a Mediterranean artichoke "ragout" and smothered in Classic Pesto (page 137) and Sun-dried Tomato Pesto (page 191). You don't have to use artichokes; fresh zucchini makes a nice substitution. You need to use a lot of bowls and pans to make this, so don't say I didn't warn you. It's a cute little dish, though, and worth all the futzing.

PREPARE THE ARTICHOKES:

In a large skillet over medium heat, sauté the onion in the oil until translucent, about 3 minutes. Add the garlic and cook for 1 minute more. Add the thyme, salt, pepper, and tomatoes and cook until the tomatoes have broken down and released their juices, about 5 minutes. Add the artichoke hearts, olives, and capers; simmer for 10 minutes. Add the basil and cook for 1 minute more. Turn off the heat and cover to keep warm.

PREPARE THE EGGPLANT:

Have ready a flattened paper bag or paper towels to drain the oil.

In a broad bowl, whisk the cornstarch with 1 cup of water until dissolved. Fill a dinner plate with the flour. Onto another plate, sift together the panko, herbs, salt, and pepper. Line up the dishes as follows: flour, cornstarch mixture, panko mixture.

Heat a little over ¼ inch of oil in a heavy-bottomed skillet over medium heat. Dip an eggplant slice in the flour, then in the cornstarch mixture, and then in the panko mixture, flipping to coat. When you have dipped four slices, use tongs to place them in the oil and cook until lightly browned, about 3 minutes. Flip over and cook 1 to 2 minutes more. Transfer to the paper to drain and proceed with the remaining eggplant slices.

ASSEMBLE THE LAYERS:

Pour some of the sauce you are using onto the plate. Place an eggplant slice on the sauce, then a layer of the artichokes, then an eggplant slice, then another layer of the artichokes. Add one final eggplant slice and top with sauce.

Fizzle says:

Some will say that sprinkling eggplant with salt removed the bitterness, although I am not convinced it is a wholly necessary step, because some eggplant is bred to be less bitter. If you would like to try it for yourself, sprinkle the eggplant slices with salt and set on paper towels for half an hour. Rinse the salt off the eggplant, pat dry, and proceed with the recipe.

COOKIES and BARS

Whenever I want to say "thank you" to people, I bake them cookies, or at least I think of doing it. Sometimes I bake the cookies and just eat them myself and then send an e-mail with dancing bunnies to thank the people instead. This is the chapter you're gonna want to have open on your countertop during the holidays, and during finals week and during a *Twilight Zone* marathon and . . . well, okay, always have it open.

<<< CRANBERRY—WHITE CHOCOLATE
BISCOTTI, PAGE 217

SPARKLED GINGER COOKIES

4 tablespoons turbinado sugar (regular sugar will work as well but coarse is best)

½ cup canola oil

¼ cup molasses

¼ cup unsweetened almond milk (or preferred nondairy milk)

1 cup granulated sugar

1 teaspoon pure vanilla extract

2 cups all-purpose flour

1 teaspoon baking soda

¼ teaspoon salt

2½ teaspoons ground ginger

½ teaspoon ground cinnamon

½ teaspoon ground cloves

Maybe these chewy, spicy sweet cookies are good any time of the year, but I like to save them for the holidays. They make me nostalgic for the snowy winter days at Grandma's cabin, sitting around the fireplace in our flannels singing . . . okay, fine, my grandma didn't have a cabin. There was no fireplace, no flannels, but these cookies sure make me wish there had been.

Preheat the oven to 350°F. Lightly grease two cookie sheets. Place the turbinado sugar in a small bowl.

In a large mixing bowl, mix together the oil, molasses, milk, granulated sugar, and vanilla. Sift the dry ingredients (flour, baking soda, salt, and spices) into the wet and mix well with a hand mixer or strong fork. Roll into 1-inch balls, flatten each into a 1½-inch-diameter disk, press the cookie tops into the turbinado sugar, and place 1 inch apart, sugar side up, on the prepared cookie sheets. Bake for 10 to 12 minutes, let cool on the cookie sheets for 3 to 5 minutes, then transfer to a cooling rack.

CHOCOLATE CHIP COOKIES

1 cup refined coconut oil, at room temperature

¾ cup granulated sugar

½ cup light brown sugar

2 tablespoons unsweetened almond milk (or preferred nondairy milk)

2 teaspoons pure vanilla extract

2½ cups all-purpose flour

1 teaspoon baking soda

1 teaspoon salt

1½ cups vegan semisweet chocolate chips

These have gone through a slight transformation since the first edition. I tried to keep the ingredients as simple as possible while still providing that ooey-gooey interior and crispy buttery exterior. Once again, coconut oil provides the buttery goodness, and everything else is just classic cookie stuff: vanilla, semisweet chocolate chips, oh, and don't forget the love.

Preheat the oven to 350°F.

In a large mixing bowl, use an electric hand mixer to cream together the oil and sugars until fluffy. Mix in the milk and vanilla. Sift in the flour, baking soda, and salt, and mix well. Fold in the chocolate chips. Drop by teaspoonfuls spaced a little over 2 inches apart onto ungreased cookie sheets. Bake for 8 to 10 minutes, until ever so slightly browned. Let cool on the baking sheets for 5 minutes, then transfer to a cooling rack.

MAPLE WALNUT COOKIES

½ cup canola oil

¼ cup pure maple syrup

2 tablespoons molasses

1 teaspoon pure vanilla extract

2 teaspoons maple extract

¾ cup sugar

¼ cup unsweetened almond milk (or preferred nondairy milk)

2 tablespoons organic cornstarch

1½ cups all-purpose flour

¾ teaspoon salt

1 teaspoon baking soda

1½ cups coarsely chopped walnuts

3 dozen walnut halves

You have to get with me on the maple walnut combination. I feel like it's sadly neglected in the catalog of autumnal treats. Let's change this! This cookie is like a trip through the beautiful mountains of Vermont at peak foliage season.

Preheat the oven to 350°F. Lightly grease three cookie sheets or line them with parchment paper.

Combine the oil, maple syrup, molasses, vanilla and maple extracts, and sugar in a mixing bowl and mix with an electric hand mixer or strong fork until well combined. The oil will separate a little but that's okay. Add the milk and cornstarch and mix until the cornstarch is well incorporated and the mixture resembles caramel.

Sift in the flour, salt, and baking soda. Mix with a wooden spoon until well combined. Fold in the chopped walnuts.

Drop by tablespoonfuls about 2 inches apart onto the prepared cookie sheets. Press a walnut half into the center of each cookie. Bake for 8 to 10 minutes. Remove from the oven, let sit for 2 minutes, then transfer to a cooling rack.

PUMPKIN OATMEAL COOKIES

2 cups all-purpose flour

1⅓ cups rolled oats

1 teaspoon baking soda

¾ teaspoon salt

1 teaspoon ground cinnamon

½ teaspoon ground nutmeg

1⅔ cups sugar

⅔ cup canola oil

2 tablespoons molasses

1 cup canned pure pumpkin
or cooked pureed pumpkin
(do not use pumpkin pie mix)

1 teaspoon pure vanilla extract

1 tablespoon ground flaxseeds

1 cup walnuts, finely chopped

½ cup raisins

These are little puffy, pitch-perfect pillows of pumpkin. Sort of wholesome, with the oats and flaxseeds, but still altogether a treat. They're soft right out of the oven, but as they cool they are nice and chewy. They taste even better the next day!

They make a lot (four dozen!), so you can totally feel free to halve the recipe.

Preheat the oven to 350°F. Lightly grease two cookie sheets.

Mix together the flour, oats, baking soda, salt, and spices.

In a separate bowl, use an electric hand mixer to mix together the sugar, oil, molasses, pumpkin, vanilla, and flaxseeds until very well combined. Add the dry ingredients to the wet in three batches, folding to combine.

With the last addition, fold in the walnuts and raisins.

Drop by tablespoons onto the prepared cookie sheets. They don't spread very much, so they can be placed only an inch apart. Flatten the tops of the cookies a bit with your fingers. Bake for 14 to 16 minutes.

Remove from the oven, cool on the cookie sheets for 2 minutes, then transfer to a cooling rack.

Fizzle says:

Want to be even more of a rockstar pastry chef? Skip the preground nutmeg and use a Microplane grater to freshly grate nutmeg into the batter instead.

BIG GIGANTOID CRUNCHY PEANUT BUTTER—OATMEAL COOKIES

MAKES ABOUT 12 HUGE COOKIES

2 cups all-purpose flour

2 cups rolled oats

2 teaspoons baking powder

1 teaspoon salt

¾ cup canola oil

¾ cup chunky all-natural peanut butter

1 cup granulated sugar

1 cup light brown sugar

½ cup unsweetened almond milk (or preferred nondairy milk)

2 teaspoons pure vanilla extract

Peanut butter fans, be on high alert. These cookies are as big as your face (well, almost) and as peanutty as can be. They're wonderfully chewy and perfect for those days when you know that one little simply won't do.

Preheat the oven to 350°F. Lightly grease two cookie sheets.

Toss together the flour, oats, baking powder, and salt in a large mixing bowl. In a separate bowl, use a strong fork to mix together the oil, peanut butter, sugars, milk, and vanilla.

Add the dry ingredients to the wet, and mix well. The dough will be very firm and moist. For perfectly round, large cookies: pack a ⅓-cup measuring cup with dough, pop out and roll the dough into a firm ball, and flatten just barely on a prepared cookie sheet, spacing the dough balls well apart. Lightly grease the bottom of a flat plate and then press the top of the cookies with the bottom of the plate to flatten to a ½-inch thickness. Leave about an inch between the flattened cookies, as these will spread slightly. Bake for 12 to 15 minutes, until the cookies have puffed a bit and are lightly browned. Allow to cool for at least 10 minutes to firm up before moving off the cookie sheet.

Fizzle says:

Love a sweet and salty combo? Go ahead and use salted peanut butter here; no one will stop you. Also, if you'd like to make normal-size cookies, use 2 tablespoons of dough instead, baking these 8 to 10 minutes.

⅓ cup refined coconut oil

½ cup smooth all-natural peanut butter (try to get the no-stir kind if you can find it; if you cannot, then stir like crazy so that the pb isn't clumpy)

2 tablespoons unsweetened almond milk (or preferred nondairy milk)

¾ cup sugar

1 teaspoon pure vanilla extract

2 tablespoons molasses (not blackstrap)

1¼ cups all-purpose flour

2 tablespoons organic cornstarch

½ teaspoon baking powder

½ teaspoon salt

The classic, homey, crosshatched top in a light and delicate shortbread cookie. The ultimate lunchbox treat, these are melt-in-your-mouth peanut buttery. This recipe originally appeared in *Vegan Cookies Invade Your Cookie Jar*; now, even better, made with coconut oil!

Preheat the oven to 350°F. Lightly grease two cookie sheets

In a large mixing bowl, beat together the oil, peanut butter, almond milk, and sugar until light and fluffy. This can take up to 2 minutes with an electric hand mixer at medium speed, or 4 minutes just using a fork. Mix in the vanilla and molasses.

Add half of the flour along with the cornstarch, baking powder, and salt and mix well. Add the remaining flour and mix. Use your hands at this point to really work the ingredients together. The dough should hold together when squeezed (see Fizzle says).

Roll the dough into walnut-size balls and flatten a bit with the palms of your hand. The dough may crack on the edges and that is fine. Place on the prepared cookie sheets. Flatten the cookies with the bottom of a coffee mug. Use the underside of fork tines to press crosshatches into the cookies, one press horizontal and one vertical.

Bake for 10 to 12 minutes, until the edges are very lightly browned. Remove from the oven and let cool on the sheets for 10 minutes; any sooner and they might crumble. Use a thin, flexible spatula to transfer the cookies to a cooling rack to cool completely.

Fizzle says:

The idea here is to limit the amount of liquid you use, but because peanut butter moisture varies from brand to brand and other mysterious cookie happenings, your dough might be dry. If it is, add 1 tablespoon or two of extra milk to the dough if it doesn't seem to be coming together.

OATMEAL RAISIN COOKIES

⅓ cup unsweetened almond milk (or preferred nondairy milk)

2 tablespoons ground flaxseeds

⅔ cup light brown sugar

⅓ cup canola oil

1 teaspoon pure vanilla extract

¾ cup all-purpose flour

½ teaspoon ground cinnamon

⅛ teaspoon ground nutmeg

¼ teaspoon baking soda

¼ teaspoon salt

1½ cups rolled oats

½ cup raisins

No one really knows where or how these humble ingredients came together to form the power couple of the cookie world, but we'll just have to chalk it up as one of life's happy little miracles. We first introduced these in *Vegan Cookies Invade Your Cookie Jar*—and they are just as awesome now.

Preheat the oven to 350°F. Line two baking sheets with parchment paper.

In a large mixing bowl, use a fork to vigorously mix together the milk and flaxseeds. Add the brown sugar and oil and mix until it resembles caramel, about 2 minutes. Mix in the vanilla.

Sift in the flour, spices, baking soda, and salt, mixing them in as they are added. Fold in the oats and raisins.

Drop the dough in generous table-spoonfuls about 2 inches apart onto the baking sheets. Flatten the tops a bit, as they don't spread much.

Bake for 10 to 12 minutes. Let cool on the sheet for 5 minutes, then transfer to a cooling rack to cool completely.

Fizzle says:

Some people prefer a chewy oatmeal raisin cookie and some prefer crunchy, so here's a little secret: 10 minutes in the oven will get you your chewy cookies and 12 minutes will get you your crunchies.

BUTTERY LEMON CUTOUT COOKIES

¾ cups refined coconut oil,
at room temperature

3 tablespoons unsweetened
applesauce

¾ cups confectioners' sugar, sifted

1½ cups all-purpose flour

1 teaspoon pure vanilla extract

2 tablespoons finely grated
lemon zest

¼ teaspoon salt

Granulated sugar for sprinkling on
the tops

Y ou can decorate these lemony delights with the simple White Icing (page 238); use a pastry bag to make swirly or stripy shape, or simply sprinkle them with some sugar.

In a mixing bowl, beat together the coconut oil, applesauce, and confectioners' sugar until light and fluffy. Add the flour in two batches, beating well after each addition. Add the remaining ingredients and mix well. Mold the dough into a disk, wrap in plastic wrap, and refrigerate for at least 2 hours, until firm.

Preheat the oven to 325°F. Line two baking sheets with parchment paper.

Roll out the dough on a lightly floured surface. Cut with 2-inch cookie cutters (heart and star shapes are awesome). Place the dough scraps in the fridge and roll them out again to make more cookies. Place the cookies 1 inch apart on the prepared baking sheets, sprinkle with granulated sugar, and bake for 6 to 8 minutes. Let cool on the baking sheets for 2 minutes, then transfer to cooling racks to cool completely.

FOR THE DOUGH:

⅔ cup refined coconut oil,
at room temperature

⅔ cup sugar

2 tablespoons unsweetened applesauce

2 tablespoons organic cornstarch

¼ cup unsweetened almond milk
(or preferred nondairy milk)

2 teaspoons pure vanilla extract

2 cups all-purpose flour

½ teaspoon baking powder

½ teaspoon baking soda

½ teaspoon salt

FOR THE FILLING:

1 pound dried Mission figs, chopped

¼ cup sugar

1 teaspoon finely grated lemon zest

Fizzle says:

Make the dough and filling a day in advance and assembly becomes a snap!

I wuv these cookie bar things. They are larger than your store-bought fig sandwich cookies, but bigger is better, right? They're like a li'l fig sandwich, and who doesn't want that? They're a great snack for a brown bag lunch.

Prepare the dough: In a mixing bowl, use an electric hand mixer to cream together the coconut oil and sugar. Add the applesauce and cornstarch and mix well. Beat in the milk and vanilla. Add the flour, baking powder, baking soda, and salt and mix well. Divide the dough into two portions, wrap in plastic wrap, and refrigerate for about an hour.

Prepare the filling: Combine all the filling ingredients plus ½ cup of water in a saucepan. Bring to a boil, then lower the heat and simmer for 5 minutes or so, stirring often. Let cool before assembling the cookies for baking.

Preheat the oven to 350°F. Lightly grease a baking sheet.

On a lightly floured surface, roll out one portion of the dough into a rectangle roughly 9 x 15 inches (you don't need to be too precise about it; it's okay if it's not perfectly rectangular). Divide the dough lengthwise into three equal strips. Place the three strips on baking sheet a few inches apart and divide the filling equally among the dough strips, creating a line of filling along the center with ½ inch of space on either side of the filling.

Roll out the second batch of dough to roughly the same dimensions (again, precision is not important here) and cut into three strips. Place this dough over the filling-topped one and seal the edges by lightly pressing with your fingertips. Cut into 1½-inch lengths but don't separate them. Bake for about 18 minutes, until lightly browned. Let cool on the baking sheet for 2 minutes, then cut each cookie again to separate, and transfer to a cooling rack to cool completely.

CHOCOLATE THUMBPRINT COOKIES

⅓ cup canola oil

⅓ cup unsweetened almond milk (or preferred nondairy milk)

¾ cup sugar

1 teaspoon pure vanilla extract

¼ teaspoon almond extract

1 cup all-purpose flour

⅓ cup unsweetened cocoa powder

¼ teaspoon baking soda

¼ teaspoon salt

6 teaspoons seedless raspberry jam

People love thumbprint cookies. The name and the cute little dollop of jam always elicit awwws from the masses. There's something really homey and sweet about giving the center of each cookie a little kiss with your thumb. Even if you're actually using a utensil to make the indent. These have a nice little hint of almond in the dough, which goes great with the raspberry jam.

Preheat the oven to 350°F. Line two cookie sheets with parchment paper.

In a large mixing bowl, mix together the oil and milk. Whisk in the sugar and extracts. Sift in the flour, cocoa powder, baking soda, and salt and stir well to combine.

With damp hands to keep the dough from sticking, roll 1 tablespoon of dough into a ball and press each one between your palms into a disk about an 1½ inches in diameter, then place on the prepared cookie sheet.

Continue to form the cookies, placing them 2 inches apart on the sheet. Bake the cookies for 5 minutes, then remove from the oven. Give 'em a few minutes to cool just a tad, then press your thumb (or the handle of a wooden spoon) into each cookie to make an indent. They're pretty hot at this point, so proceed carefully. Place ¼ teaspoon of jam into each indentation. Bake for another 6 minutes. Remove from the oven and let sit for 2 minutes, then transfer to a cooling rack.

CRANBERRY—WHITE CHOCOLATE BISCOTTI

MAKES AROUND 16 BISCOTTI

⅓ cup unsweetened almond milk (or preferred nondairy milk)

2 tablespoons ground flaxseeds

2 teaspoons orange zest

¾ cup sugar

½ cup canola oil

1 teaspoon pure vanilla extract

1⅔ cups all-purpose flour

2 tablespoons organic cornstarch

2 teaspoons baking powder

¼ teaspoon ground allspice

½ teaspoon salt

½ cup vegan white chocolate chips

½ cup dried cranberries

A fruity biscotti with tart cranberries, sweet white chocolate chips, a dash of orange, and a hint of allspice. In *Vegan Cookies Invade Your Cookie Jar*, we noted that this is perfect for the winter holidays or with some Lady Grey tea. Why mess with perfection? (But if you don't have holidays or tea, you can still make 'em). If you don't have vegan white chocolate chips, don't use regular chocolate chips, because they would be overwhelming. Instead use macadamia nuts, as they're nice and creamy (for a nut).

Preheat the oven to 350°F. Line a baking sheet with parchment paper.

In a large mixing bowl, whisk together the milk and flaxseeds, beating for about 30 seconds. Mix in the orange zest, sugar, oil, and vanilla. Sift in the flour, cornstarch, baking powder, allspice, and salt. Stir to combine, and just before the dough comes together, knead in the chips and cranberries. Knead to form a stiff dough. If the cranberries and chips pop out, just press them back in as well as you can.

On the parchment, form the dough into a log and press into a rectangle about 12 x 4 inches. Bake for 26 to 28 minutes, until lightly puffed and browned. Let cool on the baking sheet for about 30 minutes.

Preheat the oven to 325°F. Carefully transfer the log to a cutting board. With a heavy, very sharp knife, slice ½-inch-thick slices. The best way to do this is in one motion per slice, pushing down; don't "saw" the slices off or they could crumble. Stand the slices, curved sides up, ½ inch apart on the baking sheet; bake for 20 to 25 minutes, until the biscotti appear dry and toasted. Transfer to a cooling rack to cool completely.

KITCHEN SINK CHOCOLATE BISCOTTI

¼ cup unsweetened almond milk (or preferred nondairy milk)

2 tablespoons ground flaxseeds

½ cup canola oil

1 cup sugar

2 teaspoons pure vanilla extract

1½ cups all-purpose flour

½ cup Dutch-processed cocoa powder

1¼ teaspoons baking powder

¼ teaspoon salt

**MIX-IN IDEAS
(USE UP TO 1 CUP TOTAL):**

Vegan chocolate chips and chopped walnuts

Dried cherries and vegan white chocolate chips

Chopped macadamias and candied ginger

Chopped peanuts and raisins

Chopped hazelnuts and cacao nibs

I'm a huge biscotti fan. What's not to love about basically baking up one huge cookie, then transforming it into a bunch of crisp cookie fingers built for dunking into tea, coffee, or almond milk? First introduced in *Vegan Cookies Invade Your Cookie Jar*, here is my favorite all-purpose chocolate biscotti that's ideal for those times when you can't decide what to put in your biscotti. Peanuts? Chocolate chips? How about everything? The dough can support up to 1 generous cup of mix-ins, depending on the actual size and shape. Just press back into the dough log any bits and pieces that should pop out during the kneading process.

Preheat the oven to 350°F. Line baking sheets with parchment paper.

In a large mixing bowl, beat together the milk and ground flaxseeds until smooth. Add the oil, sugar, and vanilla and mix to combine.

Sift in the flour, cocoa powder, baking powder, and salt. Stir to form a smooth dough, then knead in up to 1 cup of mix-ins, pushing any pieces that pop out back into the dough.

Form a log about 10 x 4 inches, using a rubber spatula to even the edges and flatten the ends of the log. Bake for 30 minutes, or until the log is puffed and firm. Some cracking is okay. Place the baking sheet on a cooling rack, turn off the oven, and allow the log to cool for at least 45 minutes. If any edges of the log are too browned, gently trim off with a sharp, heavy knife.

Preheat the oven to 325°F. Very carefully slide the log off its baking sheet onto a cutting board. With a sharp, heavy knife, slice the log into ½-inch-thick slices, using one quick and firm motion per slice, pressing down into the log. Very gently move the slices back to the baking sheet, standing the slices on their bottom edge if possible. Bake the slices for 26 to 28 minutes. The slices should appear dry, and any nuts that show should be lightly toasted. Allow to cool for 10 minutes on the baking sheet, then carefully transfer to cooling racks to cool completely (warm cookies may be fragile). Store in a loosely covered container.

BANANA SPLIT PUDDING BROWNIES

FOR THE BROWNIES:

4 ounces vegan semisweet chocolate, chopped

1 cup mashed very ripe banana (about 2 large bananas)

⅓ cup canola oil

1 cup sugar

1 teaspoon pure vanilla extract

¾ cup all-purpose flour

¼ cup unsweetened cocoa powder

¼ teaspoon baking soda

⅛ teaspoon salt

FOR THE TOPPING LAYER:

1 cup mashed very ripe banana (about 2 large bananas)

2 tablespoons sugar

¼ cup unsweetened almond milk (or preferred nondairy milk)

½ teaspoon pure vanilla extract

1 tablespoon organic cornstarch

For decoration and more banana yumminess:

1 ripe but not very ripe banana, thinly sliced

2 tablespoons freshly squeezed lemon juice

This is a really fudgy brownie with a banana pudding on top that melts into the brownie layer and forms this unbelievable ooey-gooey banana brownie concoction. Although you *can* hold it in your hand, you may want to serve it with a fork.

Preheat the oven to 350°F. Spray a 9 x 13-inch baking pan with nonstick cooking spray or very lightly grease with oil.

Prepare the brownie layer: Melt the chocolate by placing in a pan or heat-proof mixing bowl over a small pot of boiling water. Stir with a heatproof spatula until completely melted, then remove from the heat and set aside to cool.

In a large mixing bowl, combine the mashed banana, oil, and sugar. Use an electric hand mixer to beat everything together for about a minute. If you don't have a mixer, use a strong fork and mix for about 3 minutes. Mix in the vanilla and melted chocolate.

Sift in the flour, cocoa powder, baking soda, and salt, mixing with the hand mixer as you go along. Mix until smooth.

Prepare the banana layer: In a small bowl, combine all the topping ingredients and mix with the hand mixer (remember to rinse the beaters off first) for about a minute.

Spread the brownie batter evenly into baking pan with a rubber spatula. Pour the banana topping over that and spread evenly. Bake for 30 to 35 minutes; the top should be lightly browned. Remove from the oven and let cool. After it's cooled down a bit, move it to the fridge to chill completely.

When ready to serve, toss the sliced bananas in lemon juice in a small bowl. Cut the baked cake into twelve squares, place a few slices of banana on top of each portion, and serve.

DELUXE COCOA BROWNIES

3 ounces firm silken tofu, such as Mori-nu (¼ of the package)

¼ cup unsweetened almond milk (or preferred nondairy milk)

½ cup canola oil

1 cup sugar

2 teaspoons pure vanilla extract

1 cup all-purpose flour

½ cup unsweetened cocoa powder

1 tablespoon organic cornstarch

½ teaspoon baking powder

½ teaspoon salt

VARIATIONS:

Add 1 cup of chopped walnuts

Add ¾ cup of vegan chocolate chips

Originally from *Vegan Cookies Invade Your Cookie Jar*: Brownie purists will delight in these supermoist, melt-in-your-mouth, rich cocoa brownies. These are somewhere between fudgy and cakey, reminiscent of a brownie box mix. It is important to sift in the dry ingredients with a sifter. Clumpy cocoa or cornstarch can ruin your precious brownie, so sift!

Preheat the oven to 325°F. Line an 8-inch square brownie pan with parchment paper; it should cover the bottom as well as curve up and cover the sides.

Puree the tofu, milk, and oil in a blender or food processor until smooth and fluffy. Use a spatula to scrape down the sides to make sure you get everything.

Transfer to a mixing bowl. Use a fork to vigorously mix in the sugar. Add the vanilla.

Sift in the flour, cocoa powder, cornstarch, baking powder, and salt. Use a spatula to fold and mix the batter until smooth. Transfer the batter to the prepared pan and smooth out the top. It's okay if the batter doesn't sink all the way into the sides and edges of pan; it will spread during baking. Bake for 30 to 32 minutes, until the mixture pulls away from the sides of the pan. Remove from the oven, and let cool for at least 15 minutes before slicing into twelve bars before serving.

CALL ME BLONDIES

3 ounces firm silken tofu, such as Mori-nu (¼ of the package)

¼ cup unsweetened almond milk (or preferred nondairy milk)

⅓ cup canola oil

½ cup light brown sugar

½ cup granulated sugar

1 teaspoon pure vanilla extract

1½ cups all-purpose flour

½ teaspoon baking soda

¼ teaspoon baking powder

½ teaspoon salt

¾ cup vegan semisweet chocolate chips

VARIATIONS:

These really are a great base for almost any combo you can imagine. Try ¾ cup of vegan white chocolate chips and ¾ cup of macadamia nuts. Or ¾ cup of walnuts in addition to the chocolate chips.

I'm no music historian, but could it be that Deborah Harry named her band after this chewy, gooey bar? This is a nice and easy basic blondie who originally called to us in *Vegan Cookies Invade Your Cookie Jar*, quick to throw together and packed with chocolate chips. The secret to the texture is not to overbake; once the edges are lightly browned, these babies are done.

Preheat the oven to 325°F. Line an 8-inch square brownie pan with parchment paper; it should cover the bottom as well as curve up and cover the sides.

Puree the tofu, milk, and oil in a blender or food processor until smooth and fluffy. Use a spatula to scrape down the sides to make sure you get everything.

Transfer to a mixing bowl. Use a fork to vigorously mix in the sugars. Add the vanilla.

Sift in the flour, baking soda, baking powder, and salt. Use a spatula to fold and mix the batter until smooth. Fold in the chocolate chips (and any other ingredients, if you are making a variation). Transfer the batter to the prepared pan and smooth out the top. It's okay if the batter doesn't sink all the way into the sides and edges of pan; it will spread a bit during baking. Bake for 27 to 30 minutes; the sides should be just slightly browned. Remove from the oven and let cool for at least 30 minutes before slicing into twelve bars and serving.

MACADAMIA BLONDIES
WITH CARAMEL–MAPLE TOPPING

MAKES 16 BLONDIES

FOR THE BLONDIES:

2¾ cups all-purpose flour

1 teaspoon baking powder

1 teaspoon baking soda

½ teaspoon salt

6 ounces firm silken tofu
(the vacuum-packed kind)

¼ cup unsweetened almond milk
(or preferred nondairy milk)

⅓ cup canola oil

2 cups granulated sugar

2 tablespoons pure vanilla extract

1¼ cups raw macadamias, partially
chopped and partially ground (see
Fizzle says)

FOR THE TOPPING:

¼ cup refined coconut oil

2 tablespoons light brown sugar

¼ cup pure maple syrup

1 cup raw macadamia nuts,
coarsely chopped

Macadamias make these blondies rich and buttery. They're a sweet, decadent treat that always goes over really well at a potluck, provided you have plenty of napkins.

Preheat the oven to 350°F. Lightly grease a 9 x 13-inch baking pan.

Prepare the dough: In a large mixing bowl, sift together the flour, baking powder, baking soda, and salt.

In a blender, whiz the tofu with the milk until smooth. Add the oil, granulated sugar, and vanilla, and blend again.

Fizzle says:

For the bestest texture, the macadamias should be partially ground and partially chopped, which is achieved in a food processor with about thirty pulses. If you don't have a food processor, then chop all the macadamias, put half of them aside, and continue to chop the others or grind them in a blender until they resemble coarse crumbs.

Pour the tofu mixture into the flour mixture and use a strong fork or an electric hand mixer to combine until smooth. Fold in the macadamias. The batter will be thick and have a cookie dough consistency. Spread in the baking pan and bake for 25 minutes.

Meanwhile, prepare the topping: In a saucepan over medium heat, combine the oil, brown sugar, and maple syrup, and heat until the sugar dissolves. Increase the heat to bring to a boil, and boil for 1 minute. Stir in the nuts. Remove from the heat.

Remove the blondies from the oven and pour the topping over them, return to the oven, and bake for 15 more minutes, until the topping is really bubbly.

Let cool completely before serving; the topping should harden to a caramel-like consistency. Slice into sixteen squares, or get fancy and slice into triangles.

RASPBERRY—CHOCOLATE CHIP BLONDIE BARS

MAKES 16 BARS

FOR RASPBERRY LAYER:

2 cups frozen raspberries

3 tablespoons organic cornstarch

¼ cup cold water

⅓ cup sugar

FOR THE BLONDIE LAYER:

1 (6-ounce) container plain or vanilla vegan yogurt

¼ cup unsweetened almond milk (or preferred nondairy milk)

½ cup plus 2 tablespoons canola oil

2 cups sugar

1 tablespoon pure vanilla extract

3¾ cups all-purpose flour

1¼ teaspoons baking soda

½ teaspoon salt

1 cup vegan semisweet chocolate chips

These are blondies topped with a raspberry spread and chocolate chips, then finished off with some of the blondie batter dolloped on top. They're tantalizing and cool looking and kids seem to really enjoy them. Maybe it's all the pretty red peeking through or maybe it's the chocolate chips? Adults won't argue with one of these bars, either.

Preheat the oven to 350°F. Lightly grease a 9 x 13-inch baking pan.

Prepare the raspberry layer: In a saucepan, combine all raspberry layer ingredients and stir until the cornstarch is dissolved. Bring to a boil and then lower the heat to a simmer. Cook, stirring often, for 5 minutes, or until thickened. Remove from the heat, but keep covered and warm.

Prepare the blondie layer: In a large mixing bowl, combine the yogurt, milk, oil, sugar, and vanilla. Mix until well combined. Sift in the flour, baking soda, and salt, mixing as you go. Mix until relatively smooth. Set aside 1 cup of the dough and spread the rest in the prepared baking pan. Spread the raspberry layer over the dough. Sprinkle half of the chocolate chips over the raspberry layer. Dollop the remaining dough over the chips and raspberries; sprinkle the rest of the chocolate chips over that. Bake for 35 minutes. Let cool completely before slicing into sixteen bars and serving.

Fizzle says:

If you are low on time, you can use 1 cup of raspberry preserves or jam in place of the raspberry layer.

DATE-NUT DIAMONDS

1 cup all-purpose flour

⅛ teaspoon salt

½ cup refined coconut oil,
at room temperature

¾ cup dried dates, roughly chopped

¾ cup light brown sugar

1 cup chopped walnuts

½ cup unsweetened shredded
coconut

1 teaspoon pure vanilla extract

2 tablespoons tapioca starch

Okay, you don't have to cut these into diamonds, but they look cute if you choose to. These bars are very *Home and Garden*. In fact, I'm pretty sure I stole the recipe from that magazine years and years ago. They're very nutty and cozy, with the dates, walnuts, brown sugar, and coconut.

Preheat the oven to 375°F. Lightly grease an 11 x 17-inch baking sheet.

In a large mixing bowl, combine the flour and salt. Cut in the coconut oil, using a pastry knife or your fingers, until you've got coarse crumbs. Firmly press the mixture into the prepared pan. Bake for 12 minutes.

In a small saucepan, place the dates in enough water to cover. Bring to a boil, lower the heat, cover, and simmer for 10 minutes. Drain.

In a mixing bowl, stir together the cooked dates, brown sugar, walnuts, coconut, and vanilla. Sprinkle with the tapioca starch and stir until combined. Spread evenly over the partially baked crust. Bake for 15 minutes. Remove from the oven and let cool. Cut into about twenty diamonds by cutting into strips lengthwise, then diagonally.

CAKES, PIES, *and* OTHER DESSERTS

Vegan baking has come such a long way, and I am proud to have played my part in that. Gone are the days of the paperweight vegan cookie filled with nothing but oats and twigs. (Oats are delicious, but twigs are not.) We are living in a post–vegan cupcake world, where anything is possible!

If I had a nickel for every time someone told me they can cook but they can't bake, well, I'd open a vegan bakery with all that money. Get an oven thermometer, a timer, and appropriate pans; follow the recipe; and I assure you, you can bake! (And if you really cannot bake—which is just not true, but whatever—there are a couple of puddings included.)

‹‹‹ PEACH COBBLER, PAGE 256

GINGER-MACADAMIA-COCONUT-CARROT CAKE

1 cup pineapple juice

½ cup canola oil

¾ cup sugar

½ cup pure maple syrup

2 teaspoons pure vanilla extract

2⅓ cups all-purpose flour

1 tablespoon baking powder

1 teaspoon baking soda

¾ teaspoon salt

2 teaspoons ground cinnamon

½ teaspoon ground nutmeg

1 cup macadamia nuts, roughly chopped

¼ cup crystallized ginger, finely chopped

1 cup unsweetened shredded coconut

2 cups grated carrot

Fluffy White Icing (page 238)

I f I were to make a commercial for this carrot cake, it would feature a family in middle America going, "What's for dessert?" and then the mom, with perfectly coifed hair and dish towels in her hands says, "Carrot cake," and then the kids with bowl haircuts say, "Carrot cake again?" and put their face in their hands. The husband puffs on his pipe and buries his face in the newspaper, completely uninterested. But the mom's got a mischievous look in her eye; she brings out the carrot cake and suddenly there is a calypso band in the dining room and the kids start dancing; heck, even Grandma joins in the dance. What I am saying is that this is not your average carrot cake. Feel free to replace the macadamia nuts with their more affordable cousins, walnuts.

Preheat the oven to 350°F. Lightly grease two 8-inch round springform cake pans.

In a large mixing bowl, use an electric hand mixer to beat together the pineapple juice, oil, sugar, maple syrup, and vanilla. Sift in the flour, baking powder, baking soda, salt, cinnamon, and nutmeg, mixing as you go. Mix until relatively smooth, then use a rubber spatula to fold in the macadamias, ginger, coconut, and carrot.

Divide the batter evenly between the two prepared pans. Bake for 35 to 40 minutes, until pulling away from the sides. Let cool completely in the pans. Remove from the pans and put a layer of icing between the layers, and another layer of coconut icing on top; I like to leave the sides free of frosting because it looks pretty.

Fizzle says:

Don't wanna bother with a layer cake? Bake in a 9 x 13-inch sheet pan instead, and frost away with your lazy self. It takes about 45 minutes to bake.

ORANGE-RUM TEA CAKE

FOR THE CAKE:

1 (6-ounce) container plain vegan yogurt

⅓ cup canola oil

¾ cup sugar

¼ cup unsweetened almond milk (or preferred nondairy milk)

¼ cup freshly squeezed orange juice

4 teaspoons finely grated fresh orange zest

1 teaspoon pure vanilla extract

1¼ cups all-purpose flour

¼ cup finely ground cornmeal

1½ teaspoons baking powder

½ teaspoon salt

½ cup slivered almonds

FOR ORANGE RUM SYRUP:

⅓ cup freshly squeezed orange juice

2 tablespoons sugar

2 tablespoons rum

This is an intensely orange cake, perfect as an afternoon treat whilst you take tea with your other white-gloved socialite friends. There's no frosting, just a simple orange rum syrup that takes all of three minutes to put together, and it forms a nice caramelly base for the slivered almonds. You will need about six average-size oranges to get the amount of juice needed.

Preheat the oven to 350°F. Lightly grease an 8-inch round springform pan.

Prepare the cake: In a large mixing bowl, mix together the yogurt, oil, and sugar. Add the milk, orange juice, orange zest, and vanilla. Mix well to combine.

Sift in the flour, cornmeal, baking powder, and salt, mixing as you go, then mix until relatively smooth.

Transfer the batter to the prepared baking pan and bake until golden, when a toothpick or knife inserted in center comes out clean, about 35 minutes.

Remove from the oven and let cool for about 15 minutes.

While the cake is cooling, prepare the syrup: In a small saucepan, bring the orange juice and sugar to a boil over medium-high heat, stirring constantly until the sugar is dissolved. Lower the heat to a simmer, add the rum, and simmer for 2 more minutes. Remove from the heat and let cool completely.

When the cake has cooled completely, release it from the pan. Place on a serving plate and arrange the slivered almonds on top. Pour the cooled orange syrup over the top; let sit for a couple of minutes to absorb the syrup. Serve.

RASPBERRY BLACKOUT CAKE with GANACHE

1½ cups unsweetened almond milk (or preferred nondairy milk)

½ cup canola oil

1 (10-ounce) jar raspberry preserves

1¼ cups sugar

2 teaspoons pure vanilla extract

1½ cups all-purpose flour

½ cup Dutch-processed cocoa powder

1 teaspoon baking powder

1 teaspoon baking soda

½ teaspoon salt

Chocolate Ganache (page 234)

Fresh raspberries for decorating and yumminess

Deep, dark chocolate and sultry raspberries. This cake is just plain sexy. It's perfect for a birthday or for Valentine's Day or for when you've had a really rough day and just need cake.

Preheat the oven to 350°F. Lightly grease two 8-inch round springform cake pans with cooking spray.

In a large mixing bowl, use an electric hand mixer to beat together the milk, oil, ½ cup of the raspberry preserves, and the sugar and vanilla. The preserves should be mostly dissolved with the rest of the ingredients; some small clumps are okay. Sift in the flour, cocoa powder, baking powder, baking soda, and salt, mixing as you go. Mix until relatively smooth. Divide the batter between the two prepared pans and bake for 40 to 45 minutes, or until a toothpick or knife inserted into the center comes out clean. Remove from the oven and let cool in the pans.

When the cakes have cooled fully, release from the pans and place on a cooling rack over the sink (because things will get messy!). Spread the top of one cake with a thin layer of the reserved raspberry preserves (give the preserves a quick mix with a strong fork to get a spreadable consistency); spread a layer of ganache on top of the preserves. Place the other layer of cake on top and spread its top with preserves. Carefully pour the ganache over the top and sides.

Place the leftover ganache in the fridge to stiffen so that you can pipe it out. Place the cake in the fridge to set as well.

Once the ganache is chilled sufficiently to hold its shape, dot the circumference of the cake with raspberries. Place the leftover ganache in a pastry bag and pipe out rosebuds or stars or something cute between the raspberries. Place a few raspberries in the center to finish it off!

CONTINUED >>>

>>> CONTINUED FROM PAGE 232

CHOCOLATE GANACHE

¾ cup coconut milk

¼ cup refined coconut oil

10 ounces vegan semisweet chocolate chips

In a saucepan over medium heat, bring the coconut milk to a low boil. Turn off the heat and add the oil and chocolate chips, stirring until melted and completely smooth. Let sit for at least 1 hour. It should still have a pourable consistency at this point. Proceed with the recipe above.

Fizzle says:

This recipe makes a lot of ganache, in hopes that you will use it to pipe out pretty pastry bag flowers or stars. If you don't want to do that, that's cool. You can roll the leftover ganache into little truffles and dust with unsweetened cocoa powder and have an awesome extra treat.

CHOCOLATE-RUM PUDDING CAKE

1 cup all-purpose flour

2 teaspoons baking powder

½ teaspoon baking soda

¼ teaspoon salt

1 cup sugar

½ cup Dutch-processed cocoa powder

½ cup unsweetened almond milk (or preferred nondairy milk)

¼ cup canola oil

1 teaspoon pure vanilla extract

1 teaspoon rum extract (or just use 1 more teaspoon vanilla if you don't have rum extract)

½ cup boiling water

½ cup pure maple syrup

¼ cup light rum

A luscious one-bowl dessert! It's a fluffy cake with a creamy pudding layer on top, oozing chocolate all over. Serve warm or cold. It's a quick recipe that will make people think it took more work than it really did. If you are a pathological liar, just go ahead and let them think that.

Boil some water in a teakettle, preheat the oven to 350°F, and grease an 8-inch round springform cake pan.

Sift together the flour, baking powder, baking soda, salt, ¾ cup of the sugar, and ¼ cup of the cocoa powder. Make a well in the center and add the milk, oil, and extracts, and mix into a thick batter. Spread the batter in the prepared cake pan. Sprinkle the top with the remaining cocoa powder and sugar. Pour ½ cup of boiling water into a glass measuring cup, add the maple syrup and rum to the water, and pour this mixture on top of the cake batter.

Place the cake pan on a cookie sheet in case of pudding overflow and bake for 30 to 35 minutes until pudding is thick and bubbly. Let cool just a bit; while it's still warm, place the cake on a large plate and release the sides of the pan (your plate should have a slight rim to prevent spillage). Throw on a scoop of vanilla vegan ice cream, if you like, and you've got yourself one impressive dessert.

 *Fizzle says:*

Your springform pan has to be really tight for this cake to work and not leak. If it's at all bent out of shape, you might have a cake baking on the bottom of your oven. Whoops. To make sure that your springform pan is sealed tightly enough, close it up and pour some water in. If the water stays, then you're good to go! If it leaks at all, it might be time for a new pan.

PUMPKIN CHEESECAKE
with PRALINE TOPPING

FOR THE CRUST:

1¼ cups finely ground vegan graham crackers or gingersnaps

2 tablespoons granulated sugar

3 tablespoons melted refined coconut oil

1 tablespoon unsweetened almond milk (or preferred nondairy milk)

FOR THE TOPPING:

⅓ cup light brown sugar

1 tablespoon refined coconut oil

Pinch of salt

1 cup pecans, roughly chopped

FOR THE FILLING:

½ cup whole unroasted cashews, soaked in water for at least 2 hours or overnight, until very soft (see Fizzle says, page 117)

1¾ cups canned pure pumpkin puree

¼ cup mashed banana (about ½ medium-size banana)

1 (12-ounce) package silken tofu, drained

½ cup granulated sugar

⅓ cup light brown sugar

3 tablespoons refined coconut oil, melted

2 tablespoons organic cornstarch

2 tablespoons freshly squeezed lemon juice

2½ teaspoons pure vanilla extract

¼ teaspoon salt

¾ teaspoon ground cinnamon

¼ teaspoon ground ginger

¼ teaspoon ground nutmeg

Pumpkin cheesecake: two words that always get my attention, and likely yours as well. While fresh pumpkin is great for straight-up pies, I prefer the consistency and flavor of canned for this insanely popular fall dessert; plus canned pumpkin equals pumpkin cheesecake all year round. This recipe is a slightly modified version of the one appearing in *Vegan Pie in the Sky*.

Prepare the crust: Preheat the oven to 350°F and lightly spray a 9-inch round springform pan with nonstick cooking spray.

In a mixing bowl, combine the crumbs and sugar. Drizzle in the oil. Use a spoon to blend the mixture thoroughly to moisten the crumbs, then drizzle in the milk and stir again to form a crumbly dough.

Transfer the crumbs to the pan. Press firmly into the bottom. Bake for 8 to 12 minutes, until firm. Let the crust cool a bit before filling. Keep the oven on at 350°F to bake the cheesecake.

Prepare the topping: In a mixing bowl, use a fork to mash together brown sugar, coconut oil, and salt until crumbly, then fold in the chopped nuts and stir to coat the mixture. Set aside until ready to use.

Prepare the filling: Blend all the filling ingredients until completely smooth and no bits of cashew remain; a food processor or strong blender should be able to get the job done. Transfer the filling to the prepared crust.

Bake the cheesecake for 45 to 50 minutes. Remove the cheesecake halfway through baking and sprinkle on the topping. Return to the oven to continue baking. The cheesecake is done when the top is lightly puffed and the edges of the cake are golden. Remove it from the oven and let cool on a rack for about 20 minutes, then transfer to the refrigerator to complete cooling, at least 3 hours or even better overnight. To serve, slice the cake, using a thin, sharp knife dipped in cold water.

BLUEBERRY COFFEE CAKE

MAKES 16 SQUARES

FOR THE TOPPING:

¼ cup all-purpose flour

3 tablespoons light brown sugar

¼ teaspoon ground cinnamon

1 tablespoon canola oil

1 cup chopped walnuts

FOR THE CAKE:

4 cups all-purpose flour

1 tablespoon baking powder

1 teaspoon baking soda

1½ teaspoons salt

1½ teaspoons ground cinnamon

¼ teaspoon ground allspice

¼ cup canola oil

1 (6-ounce) container plain vegan yogurt

1 cup pure maple syrup

1½ cups unsweetened almond milk (or preferred nondairy milk)

1 teaspoon pure vanilla extract

2 cups fresh blueberries

In my country, coffee cake doesn't actually have any coffee in it; it's just a cake that goes well with coffee. It's got warm spices and juicy blueberries and a nutty, crumbly topping. If you don't drink coffee, have it with tea. If you don't drink tea or coffee, what in the world do you drink?

Preheat the oven to 350°F. Lightly grease a 9 x 13-inch baking pan with nonstick cooking spray.

Prepare the topping: In a medium-size mixing bowl, mix together the flour, brown sugar, and cinnamon. Drizzle in the oil a little at a time and mix with your fingertips until crumbs form. Add the walnuts and mix.

Make the cake: In a large mixing bowl, sift together the flour, baking powder, baking soda, salt, cinnamon, and allspice. Make a well in the center and add the oil, yogurt, maple syrup, milk, and vanilla. Vigorously mix the wet ingredients together, and then mix the wet with the dry just until combined. Fold in the blueberries.

Spread the batter in the prepared pan and sprinkle the topping evenly over it. Bake for 45 minutes, or until a toothpick or knife inserted into the center comes out clean. Let cool and serve!

Fizzle says:

You can substitute frozen blueberries for fresh but keep them in the freezer until the last possible moment to prevent thawing that might turn the batter purple. You'll also need to add 10 minutes or so of baking time to the mix.

FAUXSTESS CUPCAKES

FOR THE CUPCAKES:

1 cup unbleached all-purpose flour

¼ cup unsweetened cocoa powder

3 tablespoons unsweetened black cocoa powder

1 teaspoon baking powder

½ teaspoon baking soda

¼ teaspoon salt

1 cup unsweetened almond milk (or preferred nondairy milk)

¼ cup canola oil

½ cup pure maple syrup

¼ cup granulated sugar

1 teaspoon apple cider vinegar

1 teaspoon pure vanilla extract

FOR THE FLUFFY WHITE ICING:

¼ cup nonhydrogenated margarine, softened

¼ cup nonhydrogenated shortening, softened

1¾ cups powdered sugar, sifted if clumpy

1 teaspoons pure vanilla extract

1 tablespoon unsweetened soy milk

FOR THE CHOCOLATE GANACHE ICING:

⅓ cup unsweetened almond milk (or preferred nondairy milk)

4 ounces vegan bittersweet chocolate, chopped

2 tablespoons pure maple syrup

FOR THE ROYAL ICING (TO MAKE THE SQUIGGLIES):

2 cups confectioners' sugar

2 tablespoons soy milk powder

If I could only eat one kind of cupcake for the rest of my life, well, first I would wonder what I did to deserve such punishment, and then I would choose these. And I think I know someone who would agree with me—the entire country of America. These are my take on those cream-filled chocolate cupcakes with the swirls on top, whose name shall not be mentioned. They take a long time, there are many steps, but they are so worth it. Black cocoa powder is hard to find, but you need it to get the exact right flavor and color. If you can't find it, you can sub Dutch-processed cocoa, or don't sweat it; the cupcakes are still damn good. Don't skip the sifting step; the cocoa tends to clump up, and no one likes clumps. The recipe doubles really well, so go ahead and make a double batch.

CONTINUED >>>

>>> CONTINUED FROM PAGE 238

Prepare the cupcakes: Preheat the oven to 350°F. Line a twelve-muffin tin with paper liners; spray the liners with canola cooking spray.

In a medium-size mixing bowl, sift together the flour, cocoa powders, baking powder, baking soda, and salt.

In a separate large mixing bowl, combine the milk, oil, maple syrup, granulated sugar, vinegar, and vanilla, and beat at medium speed with an electric hand mixer for a good 2 minutes. Add the dry ingredients to the wet in two batches, mixing as you go. Beat for about a minute more.

Use a wet ice-cream scoop to fill each prepared muffin cup three-quarters full. Bake for about 28 minutes, until a toothpick inserted in the center of a cupcake comes out clean. Transfer to a cooling rack.

Prepare the Fluffy White Icing: While the cupcakes are cooling, prepare the Fluffy White Icing. In a medium-size mixing bowl, beat together the margarine and shortening with an electric hand mixer on medium speed until well combined and fluffy. Add the sugar and beat for about 3 more minutes. Add the vanilla and soy milk, and beat for another 3 to 5 minutes until fluffy. Chill until ready to use.

On to the Chocolate Ganache Icing: In a small saucepan, scorch the milk (bring it to a boil), then lower the heat to a simmer and add the chocolate and maple syrup. Mix with a heatproof spatula for about 30 seconds. Turn off the heat, and continue stirring until the chocolate is fully melted and the icing is smooth.

Now make the Royal Icing: Sift the confectioners' sugar into a mixing bowl. Add the soy milk powder. Add 1 tablespoon of water and stir, then add another tablespoon of water a little bit at a time until you reach a consistency slightly more solid than toothpaste. The icing should not be drippy at all; if it is, add a little more confectioners' sugar.

Assemble the cupcakes: To assemble the cupcakes, you will need two cake decorator's bags, one fitted with a large star-shaped or round tip and one fitted with small round tip (the kind you use for writing).

Fill the large-tipped one with Fluffy White Icing; fill the writing one with Royal Icing.

Poke a hole in the center of each cupcake, using your pinkie. Cram the tip of the bag with the Fluffy White Icing into the hole and squeeze to get as much icing into the center as you can, slowly drawing out the bag, until the icing fills to the top of the hole.

Wipe the excess icing off the top of the cupcake with a napkin or (if you're me) your finger.

Dip the top of each cupcake into the Chocolate Ganache Icing. Tilt the pan to add more depth to the icing for easier cupcake coating. Place all the cupcakes on a cutting board, make some room in your fridge, and put the cupcakes in there to set the ganache, about 10 minutes.

Use these 10 minutes to practice your squigglies for the tops. I use my left hand to steady my writing hand by holding onto my right wrist. Practice a bit and see what works for you.

Remove the cupcakes from the fridge and make your squiggles on the top of the ganache. Return to the fridge to set. I like to keep the cupcakes in there until I'm ready to serve them.

COCONUT HEAVEN CUPCAKES

FOR THE CUPCAKES:

¼ cup canola oil

1 cup coconut milk

⅔ cup granulated sugar

1 teaspoon pure vanilla extract

1 cup all-purpose flour

½ teaspoon baking powder

½ teaspoon baking soda

¼ teaspoon salt

1 cup unsweetened shredded coconut

FOR THE FROSTING:

3 tablespoons refined coconut oil, melted

2 cups confectioners' sugar, sifted

¼ cup coconut milk

1 teaspoon pure vanilla extract

1 cup unsweetened shredded coconut, plus more for garnish (optional)

These are a must for the coconut lovers in your life: dense coconut cupcakes topped off with fluffy coconut icing to die for, thus the name Coconut Heaven Cupcakes.

Prepare the cupcakes: Preheat the oven to 350°F. Line a twelve-muffin tin with paper liners, set aside.

In a large mixing bowl, beat together the oil, coconut milk, granulated sugar, and vanilla. Sift in the flour, baking powder, baking soda, and salt and mix until smooth. Fold in the coconut.

Use an ice-cream scoop to fill each prepared muffin cup about two-thirds full. Bake for 20 to 22 minutes; the cupcakes should be slightly browned around the edges and spring back when touched. Let cool for a bit and, when cool enough to handle, place each cupcake on a cooling rack to cool completely.

Prepare the frosting: Cream together the oil and confectioners' sugar. Add the coconut milk and vanilla and use an electric hand mixer to mix well until smooth. Fold in the coconut. Refrigerate until ready to use.

Frost when the cupcakes have cooled fully. You can sprinkle a little more coconut on top, if you like, or put a berry on them for a little color.

LEMON GEM CUPCAKES

¼ cup canola oil

⅔ cup plus 2 tablespoons sugar

1 cup unsweetened almond milk
(or preferred nondairy milk)

1 teaspoon pure vanilla extract

¼ cup freshly squeezed lemon juice

1 tablespoon lemon zest

1⅓ cups all-purpose flour

½ teaspoon baking powder

¾ teaspoon baking soda

¼ teaspoon salt

Lemon Frosting (recipe follows)

These are sophisticated cupcakes. They don't peek over the wrapper; the icing comes right to the top. Once baked, the cupcake gives off an iridescent glow, but don't worry, you are not living in a postapocalyptic world of glowing food, it's just the abundance of the lemon.

Preheat the oven to 350°F. Line a twelve-muffin tin with paper liners.

In a large mixing bowl, use an electric hand mixer to beat together the oil, sugar, milk, vanilla, lemon juice, and lemon zest.

Sift in the flour, baking powder, baking soda, and salt, mixing as you go, until smooth. Fill each prepared muffin cup about two-thirds full; bake for 17 to 20 minutes. Let cool for a bit and when cool enough to handle, place each cupcake on a cooling rack to cool completely. Frost when cooled completely.

LEMON FROSTING

3 tablespoons refined coconut oil, melted

2 cups confectioners' sugar, sifted

¼ cup unsweetened almond milk
(or preferred nondairy milk)

3 tablespoons freshly squeezed lemon juice

Cream together the oil and confectioners' sugar. Add the milk and lemon juice and use an electric hand mixer to mix well, until smooth. Refrigerate until ready to use.

CHOCOLATE PUDDING

2 cups unsweetened almond milk (or preferred nondairy milk)

3 tablespoons organic cornstarch

½ cup sugar

⅓ cup unsweetened cocoa powder

1 teaspoon pure vanilla extract

⅛ teaspoon almond extract

Pudding is the ultimate comfort food for me. This is a fast, yummy, and satisfying treat that you can make with ingredients you probably have on hand. Try the variations below, and top with Macadamia Crème (page 255).

In a small saucepan off the heat, whisk together the milk and cornstarch until the cornstarch is dissolved. Add the sugar and cocoa powder. Place over medium heat and cook, whisking constantly, until the mixture thickens, about 7 minutes. Once the mixture starts to bubble and is quite thick, turn off the heat. Mix in the extracts. Ladle the pudding into four wineglasses or ramekins, and chill in fridge for at least an hour and up to overnight. If you're leaving them in the fridge overnight, don't forget to cover them with plastic wrap once they are chilled to prevent a skin from forming.

VARIATIONS:

CHOCOLATE ORANGE PUDDING: Omit the almond extract; add along with the vanilla 1½ tablespoons of finely grated orange zest (from between 1 and 2 oranges) and 1 tablespoon of orange liqueur.

CHOCOLATE COCONUT PUDDING: Replace 1 cup of the milk with 1 cup of coconut milk, omit the almond extract, and add 1 teaspoon of coconut extract; sprinkle with unsweetened shredded coconut after pouring into wineglasses.

Also, try adding ½ cup of chopped walnuts or other nuts.

NO-BAKE BLACK BOTTOM— PEANUT BUTTER SILK PIE

MAKES ONE 8-INCH PIE

1 prepared Chocolate Cookie Piecrust (recipe follows) or vegan graham cracker crust

FOR CHOCOLATE BOTTOM:

4 ounces vegan semisweet chocolate

¼ cup unsweetened almond milk (or preferred nondairy milk)

FOR THE FILLING:

12 ounces extra-firm silken tofu, such as Mori-nu (the vacuum-packed kind)

¾ cup creamy all-natural peanut butter

1½ cups confectioners' sugar

2 teaspoons pure vanilla extract

⅔ cup coconut milk

1 tablespoon agar agar powder

1¼ cups boiling water

Peanut butter and chocolate. It's basically everyone's favorite combination, right? This pie is so creamy and decadent and never disappoints. What's more, you don't have to bake it!

Prepare the black bottom: Melt the chocolate by placing in a pan or heat-proof mixing bowl over a small pot of boiling water. When the chocolate has melted, add the milk and whisk until smooth. Remove from the heat. Pour most of this mixture into the prepared piecrust, reserving a couple of tablespoons to drizzle over the top of the pie. Transfer the chocolate-coated piecrust to the fridge.

Prepare the filling: Combine the tofu, peanut butter, confectioners' sugar, and vanilla in a blender or food processor. Blend until smooth.

In a small saucepan over medium heat, combine the agar agar with the boiling water. Stir constantly until dissolved, about 2 minutes.

You have to move quickly now to make sure the agar agar doesn't set, so make you're your piecrust is at the ready.

Add the agar to the blender and blend for about 15 seconds. Immediately proceed to the next step; don't let the filling sit around or it will set.

Pour the peanut butter mixture into the piecrust. Drizzle the remaining chocolate over the pie. Run a butter knife through the chocolate in straight lines to create a pretty pattern. Refrigerate for at least 3 hours. It's best if you can refrigerate it overnight; just remember to wrap it in plastic wrap after a few hours. Slice and serve!

NO-BAKE CHOCOLATE COOKIE PIECRUST

1½ cups vegan chocolate cookies, crushed

2 tablespoons sugar

⅛ teaspoon salt

¼ cup canola oil

1 tablespoon unsweetened almond milk (or preferred nondairy milk)

You can use any chocolate cookie here, but the closer they are to Oreo tasting, the better.

In a food processor fitted with a steel blade, or a blender, combine the cookies, sugar, and salt. Pulse into fine crumbs. Remove from the processor and pour into a pie plate. Drizzle with the canola oil and mix with your fingers. Drizzle with the milk and mix with your fingers. Press into the pie plate. Refrigerate until ready to use.

SWEET POTATO PIE with THREE-NUT TOPPING

MAKES ONE 9-INCH PIE

FOR THE FILLING:

1¼ pounds sweet potatoes

2 tablespoons organic cornstarch

½ cup granulated sugar

½ cup unsweetened almond milk (or preferred nondairy milk)

3 tablespoons refined coconut oil, melted

2 tablespoons pure maple syrup

6 ounces firm silken tofu (½ package of the vacuum-packed kind)

1 teaspoon ground ginger

½ teaspoon ground nutmeg

½ teaspoon ground cinnamon

¼ teaspoon ground allspice

⅛ teaspoon ground cloves

FOR THE GRAHAM CRACKER CRUST:

⅓ cup walnuts, toasted

⅓ cup hazelnuts, toasted

⅓ cup almonds, toasted

10 sheets vegan graham crackers

¼ cup firmly packed dark brown sugar

Pinch of ground ginger

Pinch of ground nutmeg

Pinch of ground cinnamon

Pinch of ground allspice

5 tablespoons canola oil

FOR THE TOPPING:

⅓ cup refined coconut oil

¼ cup light brown sugar

2 tablespoons pure maple syrup

⅓ cup whole almonds, toasted

⅓ cup whole hazelnuts, toasted

⅓ cup walnuts, toasted

Some people think sweet potatoes should only be a side dish and not a dessert; those people are not to be trusted so keep your distance. This is the perfect fall dessert, especially for Thanksgiving. I love the combination of the three nuts, but you can just do one if you're not feeling all that ambitious. This is one of the first recipes I ever got off the Internet and veganized, so it's close to my heart.

Preheat the oven to 375°F. Bake the sweet potatoes until tender, between 45 minutes and an hour, depending on the size.

Meanwhile, make the crust: Grind the nuts in a food processor, crumble in the graham crackers, and grind into crumbs. Add the brown sugar and spices; pulse to combine. Add the oil and pulse to moisten the crumbs. Press into a 9-inch pie plate, set aside. Lower the oven temperature to 350°F.

Make the filling: When the sweet potatoes are done, remove them from the oven and let them cool. Then puree them in a food processor or blender. Add all the other filling ingredients and puree until smooth. Pour the filling into the crust. Bake at 350°F until the center moves only slightly when the pan is shaken, about 40 minutes, covering with foil if the crust browns too quickly.

While the pie bakes, prepare the topping: Stir the coconut oil, brown sugar, and maple syrup in medium-size, heavy saucepan over low heat until the sugar dissolves. Increase the heat and let bubble for 1 minute. Mix in the nuts, coating them completely.

Spoon the hot nut mixture over the pie. Continue baking until the topping bubbles, about 5 minutes. Transfer to a cooling rack and let cool completely.

GINGERBREAD APPLE PIE

FOR THE CRUST:

1½ cups all-purpose flour

½ cup light brown sugar

1 teaspoon ground ginger

1 teaspoon ground cinnamon

¼ teaspoon ground allspice

½ teaspoon salt

1 teaspoon baking powder

⅓ cup refined coconut oil, at room temperature

1 tablespoon molasses

3 tablespoons cold water

FOR THE FILLING:

2 pounds Granny Smith apples (about 8), peeled, cored, and thinly sliced

½ cup light brown sugar

1 teaspoon ground cinnamon

¼ teaspoon ground nutmeg

¼ teaspoon ground allspice

½ teaspoon ground ginger

Pinch of ground cloves

¼ cup pure maple syrup

2 tablespoons organic cornstarch

Okay, rolling out crust is an art. Sometimes I don't feel like art, I just feel like pie. That's where this pie comes in handy! It's got a press-in crust that doubles as a crumb topping. And it combines the best things about holiday baking: Why choose between apple pie and gingerbread? You can have it all.

Prepare the crust: Preheat the oven to 375ºF. Sift together the flour, brown sugar, spices, salt, and baking powder. Add the coconut oil one tablespoonful at a time and cut in with a pastry cutter, knife, or your fingertips. Drizzle the molasses and water over the dough, mixing with your fingertips until the crumbs of dough begin to cling together. Set aside ½ cup of the dough. Gather together the rest of the dough and knead it into a ball. Press it evenly into the bottom and sides of a 9-inch pie pan and bake for 10 minutes.

Prepare the filling: In a large mixing bowl, combine all the filling ingredients, tossing the apples to coat, until the cornstarch is no longer visible.

Fill the piecrust with the apple mixture, and crumble the remaining ½ cup of dough over the filling. Cover with foil and bake for 30 more minutes. Remove the foil and bake for 20 minutes more; the filling should be bubbling and the apples should be tender. Serve warm or at room temperature.

 *Fizzle says:*

Apple corers can be a pain in the butt, so if you hate them or don't have one or both, just cut the apple as close to the core as you can. If you do use one, spray it with canola oil first to make it easier to get the core out of the corer once it's cored (say that five times fast).

OLIVE OIL DOUBLE CRUST

2½ cups all-purpose flour

¾ teaspoon salt

⅔ cup olive oil, partially frozen
(see instructions below)

4 to 8 tablespoons ice water

1 tablespoon apple cider vinegar

This has become my go-to crust. Olive oil produces a light, flaky crust with a surprisingly neutral taste. Plus, since it's made with pantry-friendly olive oil, it's a fast and convenient all-purpose crust ideal for fruit pies. The secret is to place the olive oil in the freezer beforehand, so that it becomes partially solid. This helps the fat blend into the dough in little pockets, creating the flakiness you crave.

 *Fizzle says:*

"Extra virgin," minimally processed coconut oil is a mainstay in natural foods kitchens. It is an ideal fat for a light, tender crust with a delicate coconut aroma. Since many of our pie fillings use coconut milk or oil, we like to reserve coconut oil crusts for special occasions, but you can make any crust into a coconut oil crust sensation.

Select an oil that's high quality and use when it's at a cool room temperature so it's semisolid but easy to scoop with a measuring spoon. Use as directed in any recipe that calls for shortening, margarine, or canola oil.

Prepare the olive oil: About an hour before beginning the recipe, place the olive oil in a plastic container. For best results, use a thin, light container, like the kind used for takeout food. Freeze the oil until it's opaque and congealed but still somewhat soft, like the consistency of slightly melted sorbet. If it's over-frozen, that's okay, just let it thaw a bit so that you can work with it.

In a large mixing bowl, sift together the flour and salt. Working quickly, add the olive oil by the tablespoonful, cutting it into the flour with your fingers or a pastry cutter, until the flour appears pebbly.

In a cup, mix together 4 tablespoons of the ice water with the apple cider vinegar. Drizzle in 2 tablespoons of the water and vinegar mixture and using a wooden spoon or rubber spatula, stir into the dough. Add more water, a tablespoon at a time, until the dough holds together to form a soft ball. Take care not to over-knead the dough.

Divide the dough in two. Press each half into a disc about an inch thick and place each disc between two 14-inch long pieces of waxed paper. Using a rolling pin, roll each piece into a circle about ¼ inch thick. For a more even, uniform circle of dough, roll the pin one or two strokes outward, turn the dough a few degrees, and roll a few times again and repeat. Repeat with the other half of the dough. Refrigerate the rolled dough wrapped in waxed paper until it's ready to use, or as directed in the recipe.

COSMOS APPLE PIE

Olive Oil Double Crust (page 250), rolled out and fit into a 9-inch pie plate

FOR THE FILLING:

6 cups peeled and cored Granny Smith apples, sliced ¼ inch thick (about 3 pounds)

⅓ cup light brown sugar

½ cup granulated sugar

1 teaspoon ground cinnamon

½ teaspoon ground ginger

⅛ teaspoon ground cloves

3 tablespoons all-purpose flour

Pinch of salt

FOR THE TOPPING:

2 tablespoons unsweetened almond milk (or preferred nondairy milk)

2 tablespoon granulated sugar

½ teaspoon ground cinnamon

If you wish to create an apple pie from scratch, you must first create the universe.
—CARL SAGAN

This apple pie is an homage to Carl Sagan, so relish it while you gaze out into the cosmos and think about how amazing it all is, and how amazing apple pie all is. This is probably the first pie you'll want to master and luckily it's also one of the easiest. I like to use Granny Smiths here, because they hold their shape and are tart enough to complement the sweetness and spices. A little dusting of cinnamon sugar at the end makes the pie look and taste great, and provides a nice crunch. The apples are perfectly plump and juicy and the luscious saucy filling just bursts all over your taste buds. Thank you, universe!

Preheat the oven to 425°F.

Prepare the filling: Combine all the filling ingredients in a large mixing bowl, tossing with your hands to coat the apples.

Add the filling to the prepared pie shell. Cover with the top crust, pinch edges together, trim any excess dough to about an inch, and crimp.

Prepare the topping: Mix together the cinnamon and sugar for the topping and place the milk in a small cup.

Brush the top of the pie with the milk and then sprinkle with the cinnamon sugar. Make five slits in the middle of the pie to let steam escape (a steak knife works great for this).

Bake for 25 minutes at 425°F, then lower the heat to 350°F and bake for 30 to 35 more minutes, slipping on a piecrust shield or foil if your edges are getting too browned. Place on a cooling rack and let cool for about half an hour before serving.

Olive Oil Double Crust (page 250), rolled out and fit into a 9-inch pie plate

FOR THE FILLING:

6 cups sliced peaches (see Fizzle says)

¾ cup sugar

¼ cup all-purpose flour

2 tablespoons freshly squeezed lemon juice

3 tablespoons minced fresh ginger

⅛ teaspoon salt

As soon as peach season rolls around, I don't care how hot it is; I will crank up the oven and bake up a peach pie. It's a bit of a project, sure, but watching people take their first flaky, spicy bite makes it all worth it.

Preheat the oven to 425°F.

First, score and blanch the peaches to get the skins off (see Fizzle says).

Combine all the filling ingredients in a large mixing bowl.

Add the filling to the prepared pie shell. Cover with the top crust, pinch edges together, trim any excess dough to about an inch, and crimp.

Make five slits in the middle of the pie to let steam escape (a steak knife works great for this).

Bake for about 25 minutes at 425°F. Lower the heat to 350°F, and slip on a piecrust shield or foil. Bake for an additional 30 minutes; the filling should be bubbling and the crust should be golden. Place on a cooling rack and let cool for about half an hour before serving.

 *Fizzle says:*

To prep the peaches, you'll need three things: (1) a big pot of boiling water; (2) a huge gigantic bowl for an ice bath; and (3) a slotted spoon to transfer the peaches.

To make the ice bath, fill a huge bowl with ice and cold water. Place it right next to the stove for fast transferring.

Score the bottoms of the peaches by making an X with a knife. Place them in the boiling water for one minute, then transfer them to the ice bath, using the slotted spoon. Let them cool for a few minutes, then peel the skins off, starting at the X you made at the bottom. Slice each peach in half, remove the pit, and slice into ¼-inch slices.

PEAR AND CRANBERRY TART

FOR THE CRUST:

¼ cup slivered almonds

1 cup all-purpose flour

¼ teaspoon salt

3 tablespoons unsweetened almond milk (or preferred nondairy milk)

¼ cup canola oil

FOR THE FILLING:

4 Bosc pears, peeled, cored, cut in half lengthwise, then sliced lengthwise into ¼-inch-thick slices

¼ cup sugar

2 tablespoons organic cornstarch

1 tablespoon finely chopped crystallized ginger

¼ cup fresh cranberries, sliced in half

¼ teaspoon almond extract

1 teaspoon ground cinnamon

½ teaspoon freshly grated nutmeg

Fizzle says:

To easily core pears, cut in half and use a measuring teaspoon to remove the seeds.

This is a really pretty tart, golden pears studded with burgundy cranberries. Arrange the pear slices all in the same direction for a really professional look. You'll need a 9-inch tart pan with a removable bottom for this recipe. If you don't have one, you can use a pie plate.

Prepare the crust: First toast the almonds. Preheat a large skillet over medium heat and place the slivered almonds in the pan. Toast, stirring often, until golden brown, 3 to 5 minutes. Transfer to a blender or food processor and pulse the toasted almonds to a fine powder.

In a large mixing bowl, sift together the flour, ground almonds, and salt. Drizzle in the milk and oil and stir together with a fork. Form the dough into a ball and flatten into a disk. Wrap in plastic wrap and refrigerate for half an hour.

Preheat the oven to 375°F. Place the chilled dough between two sheets of waxed paper. Roll out into a 10-inch circle. Peel off the top layer of paper and place the dough, paper side up, in a 9-inch tart pan. Remove the paper and use your fingers to press the dough into the bottom and sides of the pan. Remove any excess dough so the top edges of the dough are flush with the top of the pan.

Prepare the filling: Combine the pears, sugar, cornstarch, crystallized ginger, cranberries, almond extract, cinnamon, nutmeg, and 1 tablespoon of water. Toss gently to combine the ingredients. Layer the pear mixture in the tart shell, evenly distributing the cranberries as you go. If there is some liquid left over, pour it in as well. Cover the pan with foil and bake for 30 minutes. Remove the foil and bake for 15 minutes more. Remove from oven and let cool before serving.

STRAWBERRY SHORTCAKES

FOR THE STRAWBERRY SAUCE:

2 pounds strawberries, hulled and sliced (should come to about 7 cups)

½ cup sugar

1 tablespoon pure maple syrup

1 teaspoon pure vanilla extract

FOR ASSEMBLY:

12 Scones (page 49)

Macadamia Crème (recipe follows)

These are the first baked goods I make when spring rolls around and I have a million freshly picked strawberries. They aren't too sweet and you don't lose the strawberry essence because they aren't cooked. Just pure strawberry goodness.

Make the sauce before making the scones and crème because the strawberries need to sit for an hour.

Place all the sauce ingredients in a bowl, stirring to make sure all the strawberries are coated with the sugar. Cover and chill for at least an hour; the strawberries will develop a sauce on their own. That's all there is to making the sauce.

Split open the scones, spoon in some of the strawberry sauce (¼ cup or so per scone), cover, and dollop on some crème. Add a few more sliced strawberries to the top, serve.

MACADAMIA CRÈME

½ cup macadamia nuts

¼ cup unsweetened almond milk (or preferred nondairy milk)

¼ cup confectioners' sugar

½ teaspoon pure vanilla extract

¼ cup melted refined coconut oil

Takes five minutes to make, several hours to chill. I use this crème on puddings or on desserts with fruit toppings, including pancakes and waffles. It is easily modified by adding a touch of cinnamon or orange or lemon zest. It's not fluffy like whipped cream, but it does taste just as good. Try it on Chocolate Pudding (page 243).

In a food processor or strong blender, pulverize the macadamias to form a fine powder. Add the milk and blend to form a thick paste. Add the confectioners' sugar and vanilla, and blend again. Add the oil in a steady stream while blending. The mixture will resemble a thick liquid. Transfer to a container with a tight lid or a bowl covered in plastic wrap, and chill for several hours, preferably overnight.

FOR THE FILLING:

8 fresh peaches, peeled, pitted, and sliced (about 5 cups) (see Fizzle says, page 252)

¾ cup light brown sugar

1 teaspoon ground cinnamon

2 teaspoons pure vanilla extract

2 tablespoons organic cornstarch

FOR THE TOPPING:

1 cup all-purpose flour

1½ teaspoons baking powder

1 teaspoon ground cinnamon

½ teaspoon ground allspice

¼ cup light brown sugar, plus extra for sprinkling on crust

¼ cup canola oil

⅔ cup unsweetened almond milk (or preferred nondairy milk)

1 teaspoon pure vanilla extract

F or all the joys of pie without all the finesse . . . here comes peach cobbler! It's rustic and comforting and so very easy, anyone can throw it together and not have to worry too much about messing anything up.

Preheat the oven to 450°F and have ready a 9 x 13-inch baking dish.

Prepare the filling: Mix all the filling ingredients in the baking dish, set aside.

Prepare the topping: In a medium-size mixing bowl, sift together all the dry ingredients; create a well in the center, add the liquid ingredients, and mix with a wooden spoon until just combined. Drop by tablespoonfuls over the filling, leaving an inch or two of peaches between each spoonful. Sprinkle a little extra brown sugar over the top.

Bake for about 30 minutes, until the filling is bubbling and the top is browned.

METRIC CONVERSIONS

+ The recipes in this book have not been tested with metric measurements, so some variations might occur.

+ Remember that the weight of dry ingredients varies according to the volume or density factor: 1 cup of flour weighs far less than 1 cup of sugar.

GENERAL FORMULA FOR METRIC CONVERSION

Ounces to grams	ounces × 28.35 = grams
Grams to ounces	grams × 0.035 = ounces
Pounds to grams	pounds × 453.5 = grams
Pounds to kilograms	pounds × 0.45 = kilograms
Cups to liters	cups × 0.24 = liters
Fahrenheit to Celsius	(°F − 32) × 5 ÷ 9 = °C
Celsius to Fahrenheit	(°C × 9) ÷ 5 + 32 = °F

VOLUME (LIQUID) MEASUREMENTS

1 teaspoon = ⅙ fluid ounce = 5 milliliters

1 tablespoon = ½ fluid ounce = 15 milliliters

2 tablespoons = 1 fluid ounce = 30 milliliters

¼ cup = 2 fluid ounces = 60 milliliters

⅓ cup = 2⅔ fluid ounces = 79 milliliters

½ cup = 4 fluid ounces = 118 milliliters

1 cup or ½ pint = 8 fluid ounces = 250 milliliters

2 cups or 1 pint = 16 fluid ounces = 500 milliliters

4 cups or 1 quart = 32 fluid ounces = 1,000 milliliters

1 gallon = 4 liters

VOLUME (DRY) MEASUREMENTS

¼ teaspoon = 1 milliliter

½ teaspoon = 2 milliliters

¾ teaspoon = 4 milliliters

1 teaspoon = 5 milliliters

1 tablespoon = 15 milliliters

¼ cup = 59 milliliters

⅓ cup = 79 milliliters

½ cup = 118 milliliters

⅔ cup = 158 milliliters

¾ cup = 177 milliliters

1 cup = 225 milliliters

4 cups or 1 quart = 1 liter

OVEN TEMPERATURE EQUIVALENTS, FAHRENHEIT (F) AND CELSIUS (C)

100°F = 38°C

200°F = 95°C

250°F = 120°C

300°F = 150°C

350°F = 180°C

400°F = 205°C

450°F = 230°C

WEIGHT (MASS) MEASUREMENTS

1 ounce = 30 grams

2 ounces = 55 grams

3 ounces = 85 grams

4 ounces = ¼ pound = 125 grams

8 ounces = ½ pound = 240 grams

12 ounces = ¾ pound = 375 grams

16 ounces = 1 pound = 454 grams

LINEAR MEASUREMENTS

½ inch = 1½ centimeters

1 inch = 2½ centimeters

6 inches = 15 centimeters

8 inches = 20 centimeters

10 inches = 25 centimeters

12 inches = 30 centimeters

20 inches = 50 centimeters

ACKNOWLEDGMENTS

Thanks to my OG testers: Jennifer Philburn, Adam Nelson, Jo Scovell, Drew Blood, Chris Poupart, Carrie Lynn Reilly, Paula Gross, Justin Walsh, Dominique Ryder, Kittee Berns, and Lynda Bartram.

Thanks to editor and patience haver, Renee Sedliar

Project manager, Christine Marra

My agent and second mom, Marc Gerald

My first mom, Marlene Stewart

The Moskowitz Browns: Norah, Max, Mish, Aaron, and Angus

INDEX

<<< BLT MAC & CHEEZE, PAGE 150

HAZELNUT SCONES, PAGE 53 >>>

<<< ISA PIZZA, PAGE 142

© Randy Edwards

ABOUT THE AUTHOR

Isa Chandra Moskowitz is the bestselling author and coauthor of many books, including *Isa Does It*, *Veganomicon*, *Appetite for Reduction*, and *Vegan Cupcakes Take Over the World*. Her website, Post Punk Kitchen, is beloved by millions. Isa has been cooking up a vegan storm for over two decades and has been named favorite cookbook author in *VegNews* for seven years running. Raised in Brooklyn, New York, she now lives in Nebraska, where she brings swanky vegan comfort food to the great people of Omaha at her restaurant, Modern Love.

THEPPK.COM   +   @ISACHANDRA

ABOUT THE PHOTOGRAPHER

Kate Lewis is a New York City and Ohio-based food and travel photographer and stylist. Over the years, she has held every restaurant position from hostess, server, and bartender to chocolatier, barista, and cook. Kate's photography and styling has appeared in national publications like *Food & Wine* and *VegNews*; she's also worked with bestselling authors and on more than ten cookbooks. Follow Kate's everyday adventures on Instagram and Twitter, and visit her website.

KK-LEWIS.COM   +   @_KATE_LEWIS